vegan

Decadent (But Doable) Animal-Free Recipes for Entertaining & Every Day

LAUREN ULM
FOUNDER OF VEGANYUMYUM.COM

Health Communications, Inc.
Deerfield Beach, Florida

www.hcibooks.com

Library of Congress Cataloging-in-Publication Data

Ulm, Lauren.

    Vegan yum yum : decadent (but doable) animal-free recipes for entertaining and everyday / Lauren Ulm.

      p. cm.

    ISBN-13: 978-0-7573-1380-6

    ISBN-10: 0-7573-1380-9

    1. Vegan cookery. I. Title.

TX837.U45 2009

641.5'636—dc22

2009024376

Publisher: Health Communications, Inc.
      3201 S.W. 15th Street
      Deerfield Beach, FL 33442–8190

Photography ©Lauren Ulm
Cover design by Justin Rotkowitz
Interior design by Larissa Hise Henoch
Interior formatting by Lawna Patterson Oldfield

Contents

Chapter One: Breakfast and Brunch

Chapter Two: Main Dishes

Chapter Three: Appetizers

Vegan Yum Yum

Chapter Four: Salads

Chapter Five: Side Dishes and Light Meals

Chapter Six: Soups

Chapter Seven: Pasta

Chapter Eight: Desserts

Chapter Nine: Cheers to Delicious Drinks

Chapter Ten: Sauces, Dips, and Spreads

Introduction

When I started my blog, veganyumyum.com, in late 2006, I never dreamed it would turn into a book. In fact, I never really even imagined anyone would read the blog. I'd post a recipe with a photo, and I was absolutely dumbfounded one day when someone commented on the site to say they had made a recipe and liked it.

My original goal was that other vegans would find my recipes helpful and tasty. I certainly know what it's like to stand in front of the refrigerator without a clue about what to make. I also hoped that nonvegans would stop by, and the whole idea of vegan food, if they weren't already familiar with it, wouldn't seem so bad. I wanted nonvegans to see my food and think, "Yum, I could really go for that!" as opposed to, "Ugh, vegans."

Once people find out that my husband and I are vegan, they proceed to ask us a lot of questions (I'm sure you've fielded these questions as well, if you're vegan). Some of the questions involve ethics, factory farming practices, and hypothetical "But would you eat eggs if . . ." situations, but one question persists: *What on earth do you eat?*

While I rattle off the list, what most people usually picture is unappetizing steamed vegetables, a pile of beans with a sprig of parsley on top, and a block of wobbly tofu. They either haven't had any experience with vegan food or the experience they had wasn't a good one.

When I first went vegan three years ago, it was a bit of a mystery to me, too. I was totally amazed that you didn't need eggs and dairy for baking, and that the resulting treat tasted just as good. Or that with a little imagination and a few swaps, you could make decadent things like doughnuts, cupcakes, and a macaroni and cheese that rivaled my mom's and weren't just pathetic vegan stand-ins for the "real" versions. It was then that I became sort of obsessed with creating vegan food, both savory and sweet—recipes that would be enjoyed by even the staunchest carnivores.

Now my husband and I have a running joke; whenever I make something ridiculously over-the-top and decadent, we chow down with glee and declare as sarcastically as possible to each other, "Man, it sure sucks to be vegan! I'm so hungry and unsatisfied!"

Would I want each and every person to try a vegan doughnut and declare him or herself a vegan convert? Sure. A much more attainable goal, however, is much less dramatic. I want to provide vegans with an armory of fantastic recipes they can serve to their friends and family with pride.

If you've just gone vegan and find yourself in need of kitchen skills—fast—I want you to have a book full of step-by-step recipes that will make you feel like a pro in no time. And I'd simply like people not to cringe when I tell them the cupcake I'm offering them happens to be vegan. You don't have to be a vegan to eat like a vegan. You don't have to be a vegan to put together a vegan meal. You don't have to be vegan to like vegan food! I really, truly hope this book convinces people of these things. And, of course, if you are convinced, I hope going vegan is something that you seriously consider.

Confessions of a Vegan Foodie

Confession time: I'm not a chef, and I've never been to cooking school. All of the photographs in this book were taken by me. The food pictured here was made in my tiny kitchen and eaten by my husband and me immediately after photographing it (even if sometimes it was slightly colder by the time we finally got to eat it). I point these things out because I think it's important for you to know you can make food that looks and tastes just as good. It's all real food you can make in your kitchen, starting today. You don't need to be a chef or a food stylist to sit down to meals like these.

My point is that great food is just that—great! A lot of great food is vegan, and you can make it for yourself starting here. Bon appétit!

What to Expect When You Go Vegan

If you're thinking about going vegan, congrats! I know it seems like a big change, and it is. But it's not as hard as you think. You'll probably be curious to try the vegan versions of your old favorites. Vegan cheese, vegan milks, vegan meats. It can get expensive, and I guarantee you it'll be at least somewhat disappointing. The best advice I can give you is to focus on fresh, whole foods at first. But that doesn't mean you shouldn't give some of the specialty products a shot; you never know what you like until you try. But stay open-minded and take the time to learn how to make foods that you really love, not poor imitations of foods you no longer eat. That's the secret to being vegan and loving it.

That being said, there are a few specialty products that I can recommend that might make your transition easier.

- **Earth Balance Margarine:**

    Most margarines have whey in them. Earth Balance is 100% vegan, and in my experience, the very best butter replacement there is.

- **Silk Soymilk:**

    Everyone has their favorite soy milk. It really is worth it to try different brands to see what your favorite is. Personally, I find Silk to have the best flavor and texture, and it won't curdle in your coffee like other nondairy milks can. The refrigerated version is different than the nonrefrigerated version. Personally, I like the refrigerated one.

- **Vegenaise Mayonnaise:**

    This one is by far the winner when it comes to vegan mayo. There are other brands out there, but this is the only one I buy.

- **Tofutti Better Than Cream Cheese and Sour Cream:**

    Tofutti makes a killer cream cheese and sour cream. Other brands just don't stack up in my opinion.

- **Vegan Cheeses:**

    There are all sorts of cheeses out there. Many are pretty gross. My three favorite cheeses are Teese, Sheese, and Dr. Cow. Teese cheese is made by the Chicago Soydairy. It melts fabulously, so it's great for anything you'd normally put mozzarella on. Sheese cheese has a wonderful cheesy flavor (I love the smoked cheddar!), but it doesn't melt, so it's best on crackers or in sandwiches. Dr. Cow makes wonderful, hand-crafted nut cheeses that don't have any scary ingredients in them, perfect for a gourmet treat.

Nutritional Yeast:

I had no idea what nutritional yeast was before I went vegan. You'll find that most vegans use it and love it. Not only is it a nutritional supplement (offering a full assortment of B vitamins, including a vegan source of B12), but it also lends what most people describe as a "cheesy" flavor to your food. I disliked it at first, but now I use it quite frequently. Give it a shot on some salted popcorn as an experiment!

There are all sorts of wonderful and delicious foods out there (and in this book!) that will show you what being vegan is all about. You can be compassionate to the planet without giving up great food. It's a myth that vegan food is boring, flavorless, and uninspired. No one has to choose between compassionate living and delicious meals. You can be the best cook your family and friends know, and not in spite of you being vegan—but because you are.

chapter **one**

Breakfast and Brunch

Blueberry Waffles with Lemon Icing

I love these waffles and the inspiration behind them. One day I was out of maple syrup, so I made do with lemon icing instead; man, was it good! Spread the waffles with a little Earth Balance margarine, drizzle on some icing, and add some fresh blueberries. Maple syrup goes great, too, but the lemon icing complements the blueberries; it's definitely a nice change of pace. Plain or vanilla yogurt would work, too, but the blueberry yogurt gives the waffles a more defined, yet not overwhelming blueberry flavor. If you don't have a waffle maker, this recipe works great for pancakes as well.

If you're not planning on eating all ten waffles, make the whole batch and freeze extras. When you want waffles later, you just pop them into the toaster! I freeze them two at a time in plastic bags.

Blueberry Waffles with Lemon Icing

Makes 10 waffles

step 1 Preheat your waffle iron.

step 2 In a medium-size bowl, whisk together the flour, sugar, baking powder, baking soda, and salt.

step 3 In another bowl, whisk together the yogurt, soy milk, water, and oil.

step 4 Combine the wet ingredients with the dry ingredients, then gently fold in the blueberries.

step 5 Spray your waffle iron with a little bit of cooking oil spray and make a test waffle. Follow the instructions or your preferred directions for your waffle maker. (This recipe makes 10 waffles if each waffle uses 1/2 cup of batter. In my waffle maker, 1/2 cup of batter is perfect for a single waffle, and they cook for 10 minutes.)

step 6 To make the lemon icing, mix the powdered sugar, soy milk, lemon juice, and lemon zest in a blender until smooth. You can also make the icing without a blender if you sift the powdered sugar to make sure there are no lumps.

Ingredients

Waffles:

2 cups all-purpose flour

3 tablespoons sugar

2 teaspoons baking powder

1 teaspoon baking soda

1/2 teaspoon salt

1 container blueberry soy yogurt *(scant 2/3 cup; I prefer Silk brand)*

1 1/3 cups soy milk

5 tablespoons water

1/3 cup oil

1 cup fresh blueberries* *(see note below about using frozen blueberries)*

Cooking oil spray for the waffle iron

Lemon Icing:

1 cup powdered sugar

2 to 4 tablespoons soy milk

1 teaspoon lemon juice

Zest of 1/2 lemon

*Note: If using frozen blueberries, keep them in the freezer until the last second. Reserve 1 to 2 tablespoons of the dry mixture. When you're ready to add the blueberries, take them out of the freezer, measure them, and mix them with the reserved dry mixture. Then fold them into your mixed batter in no more than three folds. This will prevent your batter from turning a gray-purple color.

Breakfast Sandwiches

With a little creativity, you can have a fresh, savory breakfast sandwich again. Fluffy tofu-egg and maple soy tofu piled on fresh biscuits is sure to make your morning brighter.

Vegan Yum Yum

Breakfast Sandwiches

Makes 8 sandwiches

If you don't have time to make the biscuits, you may substitute premade English muffins.

Biscuits

step 1 Preheat the oven to 475°F.

step 2 Mix flour, baking powder, soda, and salt together.

step 3 Cut the margarine and shortening into the dry mixture with a pastry cutter or a fork until crumbly.

step 4 Add the soy milk into the above mixture until just combined.

step 5 Dump the dough out onto a floured surface and roll into 1-inch thickness.

step 6 Using a biscuit cutter, cut out circles of dough and place them on a parchment-covered baking sheet so that the rounds are touching. Bake for 15 to 20 minutes until golden.

Tofu Eggs

Cook the tofu eggs and maple soy tofu during the time it takes for the biscuits to bake.

Pressing Tofu 101

My favorite method for pressing tofu: Pour off

Biscuits:

2¼ cups all-purpose flour

4 teaspoons baking powder

¼ teaspoon baking soda

¾ teaspoon salt

3 tablespoons Earth Balance margarine

2 tablespoons shortening

1 cup soy milk plus 1 teaspoon apple cider vinegar

Tofu Eggs:

1 12-ounce package Firm Aseptic Silken Tofu

5 tablespoons soy milk

2 tablespoons nutritional yeast

1 tablespoon olive oil

¾ teaspoon salt

1 tablespoon tahini, scant

½ teaspoon Dijon mustard

1 tablespoon plus 1 teaspoon corn-starch

⅛ teaspoon baking powder

Vegetable oil for heating in pan

Maple Soy Tofu:

1 14-ounce block of water-packed tofu, pressed *(see next page for instructions)*

3 tablespoons soy sauce

3 tablespoons maple syrup

all excess water. Wrap the tofu in two paper towels. Then wrap the tofu in a terry cloth kitchen towel. Place a cast-iron skillet on top (or anything else that's flat and heavy and can get wet) and let it sit for 20 minutes or longer. After 20 minutes, the towel should be soaked through and the tofu nice and firm. The paper towel just protects the tofu from any lint or, um, cat hair that might be on the towel.

step 1 To make the tofu egg, mix the tofu, soy milk, yeast, olive oil, salt, tahini, mustard, cornstarch, and baking powder in a blender or food processor and blend well. The mixture should be very thick, but still blendable.

step 2 Heat a nonstick skillet (the batter will stick to anything else!) with a few teaspoons of vegetable oil in it.

step 3 Pour 1/3 cup of the batter into the hot pan, using a rubber spatula to gently spread the batter into a thin pancake. When beginning to brown, flip gently and cook on the other side. Continue to cook the tofu egg "pancakes"; stack and set aside.

Maple Soy Tofu

step 1 To make the maple tofu, press the moisture from the block of tofu and slice it into 10 thick rectangles.

step 2 Cook in an ungreased, nonstick skillet until brown on both sides, cooking in batches if necessary.

step 3 Place all of the cooked tofu back into the hot pan.

step 4 Add the soy sauce and maple syrup and cook until the sauce bubbles up and thickens into a glaze, being careful not to burn it. Set aside.

To assemble the sandwiches:

Place the tofu eggs and the maple tofu on the warm biscuits or on toasted English muffins and serve.

Vegan Yum Yum

British Lemon Maple Scones
with Clotted Cream

American scones are different than British scones. When I used to picture a scone in my head, it was triangular, fairly large, dry, crumbly, and sweet—and tasty. Imagine my surprise when I did a Google image search and saw photo after photo of scones that looked like biscuits. After some research (thank you, Wikipedia), I realized that British scones are indeed different than their American counterparts. They're less sweet, smaller, and fluffier—and indeed fairly similar to the U.S. biscuit. I had to make some. And I had to eat them with clotted cream, even though I had never tried it.

Clotted Cream:

4 tablespoons Earth Balance margarine

4 tablespoons Tofutti Better than Cream Cheese

2 tablespoons powdered sugar

Scones:

2 cups all-purpose flour

2½ teaspoons baking powder

½ teaspoon salt

Zest of 1 lemon

3 tablespoons maple syrup

½ cup soy milk

2 tablespoons lemon juice

⅓ cup Earth Balance margarine

Fresh blueberries or jam, to serve

Lemon Glaze:

¼ cup soy milk

1 teaspoon lemon juice

1 teaspoon powdered sugar

British Lemon Maple Scones with Clotted Cream

Makes 12 to 15 two-inch scones

Clotted Cream

Whisk the margarine, Tofutti Better than Cream Cheese, and the powdered sugar together. It takes some elbow grease, but within a minute or two it will be a thick, smooth cream. Let it sit out to soften a little if needed to ease mixing. Set aside at room temperature; refrigerating will make the cream stiffer.

Scones

step 1 Preheat the oven to 400°F.

step 2 In a medium-size bowl, whisk together the flour, baking powder, salt, and lemon zest.

step 3 In a different bowl, mix together the syrup, soy milk, and lemon juice.

step 4 Using a pastry cutter or a fork, blend the margarine into the dry ingredients until there are no chunks of margarine left and the mixture looks like damp sand.

step 5 Pour the wet ingredients into the dry ingredients and mix with your hands to form a soft dough. Mix just until combined, adding more flour if the mixture is too wet.

step 6 Turn the dough out onto a floured surface and roll or pat into a ¾-inch-thick slab. Using a biscuit cutter or a glass with a 2-inch diameter, cut out the scones. Press the scraps of dough together, roll out again, and continue cutting the scones until you've used up the dough.

step 7 Transfer the scones to a cookie sheet covered in parchment paper or a nonstick mat.

step 8 Make a lemon glaze by mixing together the soy milk, lemon juice, and powdered sugar. Brush the tops of the scones with the glaze before baking.

step 9 Bake for 12 to 15 minutes. If the scones aren't lightly brown after 15 minutes, transfer to the broiler for 1 to 2 minutes, watching carefully, to brown the tops if desired. Remove to a cooling rack.

step 10 While still warm, split and slather each side with the clotted cream. Add fresh berries or jam to the top and serve with your favorite tea.

Chard Florentine on Toast Points

While not the most healthful way to eat your greens, it's certainly one of the tastier ways. And hey, you technically are eating greens! My husband Stewart is not a huge fan of chard, but even he likes this. You can still taste the "chardy" flavor, but the sauce balances it well.

These are also great for a brunch or an afternoon snack, and they are an awesome way to use premade cheese sauce. If you make a batch ahead of time and keep it in the fridge, this warm and toasty breakfast is a breeze to make, even when you're half asleep. I've been known to just add raw, chopped baby spinach and skip the sautéing part altogether.

You can substitute any kind of greens you fancy, but the lighter ones, like spinach and chard, will probably work the best.

Chard Florentine on Toast Points

Makes 8 generous toast points (4 bread slices)

Cheezy Sauce (Thick Version)

step 1 Melt margarine in a saucepan over medium-low heat (not too hot!). Once the margarine is melted, add the flour and whisk (you actually need a whisk for this) until dissolved, forming a paste (like a roux).

step 2 Add the miso, tahini, tomato paste, soy sauce (or tamari), and lemon juice. Whisk well until the mixture is sort of thick.

step 3 Slowly whisk in the soy milk, making sure you don't have paste buildup on the sides of the pot.

step 4 Turn the heat up a bit. Add the yeast, salt, and pepper and whisk until thickened. Once the mixture starts to boil, it should be sufficiently thick. Keep warm while you prepare the chard and toast points.

Chard and Toast Points

step 1 Preheat the oven to 450°F.

step 2 Stack the chard leaves on top of one another, three to four at a time, and roll lengthwise. With a sharp chef's knife, slice the chard into thin strips. Without moving the chard, turn your knife 90 degrees and slice across the strips to make smaller pieces. You don't have to be exact; you just want to get the chard reasonably small.

step 3 Put 1 teaspoon or so of vegetable oil into a

Cheezy Sauce (Thick Version):

⅓ cup Earth Balance margarine

⅓ cup all-purpose flour

1 tablespoon white or red miso

1 tablespoon tahini

1 tablespoon tomato paste

3 tablespoons low-sodium soy sauce or tamari

1 tablespoon lemon juice *(or substitute 2 teaspoons apple cider vinegar)*

1 cup soy milk

⅓ cup nutritional yeast

1 to 2 pinches salt, to taste

Black pepper, to taste

Chard and Toast Points:

1 head chard

1 teaspoon oil

2 to 4 cloves garlic, sliced thin *(optional)*

1 pinch salt

4 slices good-quality bread *(I prefer sourdough)*

Paprika

large wok or large skillet on high heat. Add the chard, garlic, and salt and cook until it is much reduced in volume and stalks are tender crisp. (You should have 1 cup of cooked-down chard.)

step 4 Place the chard into the cheezy sauce and mix well. Spread on the bread slices and sprinkle unevenly (but not heavily) with paprika, which will help to create a cheezier look.

step 5 Bake for 8 to10 minutes or until toast is toasty, and then finish under the broiler for 1 to 3 minutes until browned. Let cool a minute or two before slicing or eating.

I used to buy cinnamon raisin swirl bread. One day I was eating a slice for breakfast and thought, "Why am I not making this myself?" Obviously it's easier to buy bread, but if you're up for it, it's super tasty and fun! I spent a lot of time on this recipe, so I hope it's successful for you, even if you've never attempted to make yeast bread before. (Mom, I'm looking at you.)

I weighed out the flour in this recipe to help you get more consistent results. Everyone's "1 cup of flour" varies in weight depending on your flour and your scooping technique. I reach into the bag with my 1-cup measure, get a heaping scoop, and then shake it until it's leveled off. That gets me 168 grams of bread flour per cup consistently. If you have a scale, measure one of your typical 1-cup scoops. It's good to know whether you generally scoop heavy or scoop light! Also, it's impossible to lose track of how many cups of flour you've measured if you're weighing it. Kitchen scales aren't that expensive, and they've saved me from ruining recipes more than once.

Bread

1³/₄ teaspoons dry active yeast

1 tablespoon sugar

¹/₄ cup lukewarm water *(105 to 110ºF)*

4 cups bread flour *(672 grams)*

2 tablespoons sugar

2 teaspoons salt

2 teaspoons cinnamon

1¹/₂ cups cool water *(divided into 1 cup and ¹/₂ cup)*

²/₃ cup raisins

Spice Mixture:

4 tablespoons sugar

3 teaspoons cinnamon

1 small pinch allspice *(optional)*

1 small pinch nutmeg *(optional)*

Cinnamon Raisin Swirl Bread

Makes 1 loaf

step 1 Grease a 9-by-5 inch loaf pan with vegetable oil or cooking spray and set aside.

step 2 In a small bowl, dissolve the yeast and sugar in the lukewarm water. The water should be between 105 and 110ºF (it will feel on the cool side of hot if you're not using a thermometer, or as hot as your shower water or slightly hotter). Set aside to proof. If you're new to bread making, "proofing" is the process of activating yeast by mixing it with sugar and liquid.

step 3 Meanwhile, in a large bowl mix the flour, sugar, salt, and cinnamon together with a whisk until well combined. Create a well in the middle of the dry ingredients and pour in the bubbly, proofed yeast mixture and 1 cup of water. Mix with your hands until just combined. Add approximately half of the remaining water, depending on how dry the dough is.

step 4 Turn out onto a lightly floured surface and begin kneading. It's okay if the dough looks bumpy and messy at first. Add more water if needed, but you shouldn't need more than the full 1¹/₂ cups. Knead for 1 to 2 minutes until there are no more dry bits and the flour is fully incorporated into the dough; then let it rest for 5 minutes.

step 5 While the dough is resting, wash out the bowl you made it in, dry thoroughly, and lightly oil it with vegetable oil or cooking spray. If it has been less than 5 minutes, straighten up the kitchen or check your

Vegan Yum Yum

e-mail or something. You want the gluten you've activated to relax a little, or "autolyze," if you want to use the technical term.

step 6 After the dough has rested, knead it for 4 to 5 minutes or until smooth, elastic, and not sticky. Add more flour, sprinkle by sprinkle, if the dough is still sticky. Once it is smooth and elastic, form it into a ball and set it in the oiled bowl, turning it once so the surface of the ball is oiled as well. Cover lightly with oiled plastic wrap and put it in a warm place to rise for 2 to 2½ hours. If you don't have a warm place, turn your oven on for a minute and then turn it off. It should feel warm—but not hot—inside. Let the dough rise in there. Don't forget it's in there and accidentally preheat your oven for something else!

step 7 Place the raisins in a small saucepan and cover, just barely, with water. Bring to a simmer, then turn off the heat. Let them sit for 10 minutes, which plumps the raisins and makes them juicier. Drain, pat dry, and toss with 1 tablespoon of flour to help them stick to the dough.

step 8 When the dough is done rising, it should be much larger and will dent when you poke it, as opposed to springing back.

step 9 Invert the bowl and scrape the dough out onto a lightly floured surface. Punch the dough down with your fist to deflate it. Stretch/press/roll it out to roughly 12 x 15 inches.

step 10 Sprinkle the dough evenly with the raisins and press them into the dough.

Breakfast and Brunch

step 11 Fold the dough in thirds, lengthwise. Using a rolling pin, flatten out the dough into a rectangle that that is approximately 1/2-inch thick and 5 inches wide. It shouldn't be wider than the length of your loaf pan, or it won't fit!

step 12 Sprinkle the sugar and spice mixture (see above) over the dough evenly, leaving a 1/2-inch to 1-inch border of unsprinkled dough on three sides (two long ones and one short).

Vegan Yum Yum

step 13 Starting from the short side that has no border, begin rolling the dough. The idea here is that the parts of the dough that don't have spices on them will stick together, making sure your loaf will stay together when you slice it after baking.

step 14 Place the dough roll seam side down into your greased loaf pan, cover with oiled plastic wrap, and let rise in a warm place for 1 hour.

step 15 Preheat the oven to 425°F. Place the dough in the oven and use a spray bottle to mist the top of the loaf with water, about five sprays. Spray again in 2 minutes. You can skip the spraying part, but it makes for a nice crust. Bake for 10 minutes. Turn down heat to 375°F and cover top of loaf lightly with aluminum foil if it is browning too quickly. Bake for another 20 to 25 minutes until loaf is golden brown and sounds hollow when tapped on the bottom. You may need to take the loaf out of the pan to test this, but it should slide out easily and will go right back in without trouble if it needs to bake longer—just be careful not to burn yourself.

step 16 Remove the baked bread from the loaf pan and let it cool completely on a wire rack. If you slice it too early it will fall apart. Eat it plain, toasted, or use it for cinnamon raisin swirl French toast!

Crumpets

Crumpets! They excite me so. They are part pancake, part muffin, and they're de-freaking-licious. If you've never made crumpets before, take a minute to read through Crumpet Boot Camp and Crumpet Troubleshooting (following the recipe) before starting to help ensure your success.

If this is the first time you've made crumpets, only make one crumpet at first, until you get the desired batter consistency and heat, and then begin making them two at a time.

Crumpets

Makes approximately 16 to 18 3-inch crumpets

step 1 In a small bowl, dissolve the yeast and sugar in the warm water. Set aside to proof.

step 2 Combine the flour, salt, baking soda, and cream of tartar. Add the soy milk and the yeast mixture, mixing well with a wooden spoon. Loosely cover with plastic wrap and let rise for 1 hour.

step 3 Stir the mixture down. Add more soy milk or flour if needed to get a very thick batter, but not so thick that you can't dip a measuring cup into it.

step 4 Heat a large cast-iron skillet or griddle over medium heat for 3 minutes. Turn down the heat a bit (about halfway between your medium and low setting, but closer to medium).

step 5 Grease two cooking rings with the margarine and place in the center of the skillet. Add $1/3$ cup of the batter to each ring. Cook for 9 minutes or until the tops are set (it will look translucent yellow instead of opaque white) and there are little holes scattered on the tops (similar to when you make pancakes).

step 6 Remove the rings with a pot holder, thick towel, or pair of tongs, leaving the crumpets on the skillet. Flip the crumpets, cook for 2 minutes longer, and then remove from the skillet. While the first two rings are cooling, cook the next two crumpets with two different rings. Continue until the batter is gone.

Special Equipment Needed:

Four crumpet rings (or some type of cooking rings) that are approximately 3 inches in diameter and at least 1 inch high (you can find these at kitchen stores or online).

Crumpets:

1 package dry active yeast *(.25 ounces)*

2 teaspoons sugar

$1/2$ cup warm water *(105 to 115°F)*

$2^1/_2$ cups all-purpose flour

$3/_4$ teaspoon salt

$1/_2$ teaspoon baking soda

$1/_2$ teaspoon cream of tartar

$1^3/_4$ cups soy milk

Earth Balance margarine *(to oil the cooking rings)*

Ingredients

Variation: If you're in the mood for something sweet, you can make Cinnamon Sugar Crumpets: Preheat the oven to broil. Place 4 crumpets on a cookie sheet covered with foil. Mix 1 tablespoon sugar, 1/2 teaspoon cinnamon, and a pinch of nutmeg and/or allspice together and sprinkle over the crumpets. Place in the oven 1 to 2 inches below the heating element and *watch for it to bubble,* about 1 to 2 minutes. *Take care not to burn your sugar.* Remove and serve.

Crumpet Boot Camp

Here are some crumpet facts to help you make the best crumpets ever:

- Crumpets need to cook slowly!
- Crumpets cook 90 percent through on the first side.
- The correct batter consistency is of the utmost importance, but it's easily adjusted if you goof up.

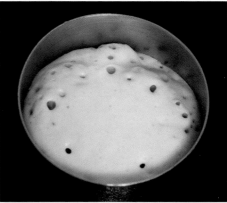

- Cast iron is highly recommended, but you can try another surface like a griddle or a nonstick skillet.
- Make sure that your rings are approximately 3 inches in diameter and at least 1 inch high.

The crumpet in this picture isn't quite ready to flip yet, but it's getting there. Once the middle looks like the edges do, you can take off the ring and flip the crumpet.

After 9 minutes of cooking, the bottom is still only golden brown. I could have let it cook longer if I wanted.

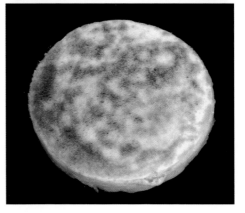

Crumpet Troubleshooting

These are some of the common problems that may occur for first-time (and seasoned!) crumpet makers:

"I don't see holes on top of my batter."
While there is a chance that your yeast didn't activate, most likely your batter is too thick. The batter needs to be thin enough to allow the gas that the yeast creates to move through it. When it reaches the surface, the bubbles break, leaving holes behind. Try adding some more soy milk to your batter. It should be thin enough that it evenly fills your rings when you pour it in. If you're moving it around with your fingers to get it to evenly fill the rings, it's definitely too thick!

"My batter is leaking out of the rings."
Your batter is too thin. Add some flour, a tablespoon at a time, until the problem resolves itself.

"The bottoms of my crumpets are scorched."
Your heat is too high. The crumpets need to sit on the skillet for 8 to 9 minutes and still be golden brown on the bottom. Crumpets should cook at a lower temperature than pancakes or crepes.

"My crumpets aren't turning golden brown."
Turn your heat up. But you knew that.

"My crumpets look fine but are gooey in the middle."
Some of mine were like this too when I ate them hot. Cook them a minute or two longer, or let them cool fully before snacking and see how that works out.

"My rings don't come off easily."
You're not greasing them enough. Use a small knife to release the crumpet and grease them better next time. The easiest way to do this is to grab a paper towel and wrap it around your extended index and middle fingers. Dip this into your margarine and rub it on the insides of your rings.

Lemon Cranberry Muffins

These muffins are light and fluffy. The lemon isn't overwhelming and goes great with the delicate almond flavor. You could substitute soy milk, but the almond milk makes for a delicious soy-free baked good.

Lemon Cranberry Muffins

Makes 12 muffins

step 1 Preheat the oven to 400°F.

step 2 Place the cranberries and water in a small saucepan and heat until simmering. Let them simmer for 3 minutes, then turn off the heat and let them stand.

step 3 In a large bowl, mix together the flour, sugar, baking powder, baking soda, salt, cornstarch, and lemon zest.

step 4 In a separate bowl (or a 2-cup liquid measuring cup), mix together the almond milk, lemon juice, vegetable oil, and the vanilla and almond extracts.

step 5 Gently fold the wet ingredients into the dry until almost combined. Drain the cranberries and fold into the batter, mixing until just combined.

step 6 Fill lined muffin tins nearly full with the batter, using as much of it as you can. (Optional: sprinkle tops with sugar. Pink muffin cups are optional, but highly recommended.)

step 7 Bake for 18 to 22 minutes or until lightly browned and a toothpick inserted comes out clean. Mine were perfect at 18 minutes. Allow to cool before serving.

Ingredients

1/2 rounded cup dried cranberries in 1/2 cup of water

2 cups all-purpose flour

1/2 cup sugar

2 teaspoons baking powder

1 teaspoon baking soda

1/4 teaspoon salt

1 tablespoon cornstarch or arrowroot powder

Zest from 1 lemon

1 cup unsweetened almond milk

Juice from 1 lemon* *(see note below)*

1/3 cup vegetable oil

1 teaspoon vanilla extract

1 teaspoon almond extract

Muffin tin lined with muffin cups

Sugar for dusting muffin tops

*Note: Lemons will vary in the amount of juice they yield. A "dry" lemon will give about 2 tablespoons and a juicy one about 1/4 cup. I've made the recipe with both dry and juicy and like the result either way. If you want a light lemon taste, 2 tablespoons will work; if you want a tangier lemon muffin, use 1/4 cup. Or do what I do: leave it to fate and use however much the lemon will give.

Strawberry Rhubarb Coffee Cake

Whoa, Mama. This coffee cake ain't messin' around. It's sweet, tangy, and moist, and the perfect way to take advantage of the bumper spring crop of strawberries and rhubarb. This makes a large 9 x 13-inch baking dish full of goodness, so invite a bunch of friends over for tea or have a luxurious Sunday brunch.

I don't peel my rhubarb when I use it, but you're more than welcome to if you want. The rhubarb cooks down in the oven, so don't worry about a chunky/crunchy end product.

One last thing: let it cool completely before trying it. I know, I know—what baked dessert tastes better at room temperature? This one. And my testers agree with me, so I'm not completely crazy.

Strawberry Rhubarb Coffee Cake

Makes 16 servings

step 1 Begin by making the filling. Hull and roughly slice the strawberries. Chop the rhubarb into 1/4-inch to 1/2-inch slices (you don't need to be precise).

step 2 Add the strawberries and rhubarb to a large pot. Add the sugar, lemon zest, and vanilla, and turn heat on low. Stir well.

step 3 Mix the cornstarch, lemon juice, and water together in a small bowl and add it to the straw-berry-rhubarb mixture, which should be very liquid by now, and turn the heat up to medium.

step 4 Stir constantly: do not step away from the pot. The mixture should be milky and light pink at first, but eventually it will become thick, transpar-ent, and dark red. After this transformation, cook for 1 minute more, then taste. It should not be gritty. If it is, cook for a bit longer to fully dissolve the cornstarch. If it tastes smooth, remove it from the heat and set aside to cool.

To Make the Cake:

step 1 Preheat the oven to 350°F and oil a 9 x 13-inch baking pan.

step 2 Whisk the flour, salt, baking powder, and baking soda together in a large bowl.

step 3 Measure the soy milk and add the apple cider vinegar to it and set it aside for a few min-utes to curdle.

Strawberry Rhubarb Filling:

3 heaping cups of organic strawberries *(about 1 pound)*

6 stalks of rhubarb, chopped into 2 inch pieces *(about 3 cups)*

1 cup sugar

Zest from 1 lemon

1 teaspoon vanilla extract

1/2 cup cornstarch

2 tablespoons lemon juice

1/4 cup water

Cake Batter:

3 cups all-purpose flour

1 teaspoon salt

1 teaspoon baking powder

1 teaspoon baking soda

1 1/2 cups soy milk plus 2 teaspoons apple cider vinegar

1/4 cup Earth Balance margarine

1/4 cup shortening

1 cup sugar

2 teaspoons vanilla extract

2 tablespoons Ener-G Egg Replacer mixed with 2 tablespoons water

Crumb Topping:

3/4 cup all-purpose flour

1/4 cup Earth Balance margarine

3/4 cup sugar

1/4 teaspoon cinnamon *(optional)*

step 4 In another bowl, cream together the margarine, shortening, and sugar until well combined.

step 5 Add the curdled soy milk, vanilla, egg substitute, and water to the creamed sugar and whisk together (it'll look totally gross!).

step 6 Add the wet mixture to the dry mixture and combine until fully incorporated, being careful not to overwork.

step 7 Scrape the cake batter into the greased baking dish, reserving 1 cup. Spread the strawberry-rhubarb mixture over the top. Use a large spoon to dollop the remaining batter on top of the filling.

step 8 Make the crumb topping by mixing together the flour, margarine, sugar, and cinnamon, using your hands, a fork, or a pastry cutter to combine until it is a crumbly texture. Sprinkle the crumb mixture over the top of the cake batter and bake for 45 to 50 minutes. Let cool completely before serving.

Stuffed Banana Berry French Toast

French toast was by far my favorite breakfast meal before I went vegan. I thought it would be impossible to make a vegan version that stood up to my memories, but it turns out it wasn't difficult at all. This recipe works equally well with unstuffed French toast, but the stuffed version sure is pretty and only slightly more of a pain in the butt. You can store any extra batter in the fridge for nearly instant French toast for a couple of days. (If you want to make this with presliced sandwich bread, feel free. I recommend mashing up the bananas and using them as a spread to keep the two slices of bread stuck together while cooking. Just be careful while flipping and it should work just fine!)

1½ cups soy milk

1 cup all-purpose flour

1 teaspoon vanilla

½ teaspoon cinnamon

⅛ teaspoon nutmeg

⅛ teaspoon allspice

1 tablespoon sugar

1 pinch salt

1 loaf good-quality, day-old bread *(I prefer sourdough)*

1 to 2 teaspoons Earth Balance margarine

1 pint strawberries, hulled and sliced

3 large, firm but ripe bananas *(little brown spots just starting)*, sliced

1 pint blackberries, raspberries, or blueberries

Strawberry sauce *(optional; see recipe below)*

Maple syrup, to serve

Powdered sugar, to serve

Strawberry Sauce:

1 cup sliced strawberries

¼ cup powdered sugar *(plus a dusting more for garnish)*

¼ teaspoon orange extract *(use a different flavor if you prefer)*

Stuffed Banana Berry French Toast

Makes 6 servings

step 1 Whisk the soy milk, flour, vanilla, cinnamon, nutmeg, allspice, sugar, and salt together in an 8 x 8-inch brownie pan (or other wide pan with high sides) until frothy. Set aside.

step 2 Slice ¾-inch slices of bread from your loaf. Slice each slice in half again, without cutting all the way through, to form a pocket. Place the bread into the batter, letting it sit for a few minutes.

step 3 While the bread is soaking, heat a nonstick pan or cast-iron griddle over medium heat. Melt a teaspoon or two of margarine on it. When the margarine begins to bubble, the pan is ready.

step 4 Take the bread out of the batter and place a few strawberries and bananas in the back of the pocket to crack it open a bit. You'll fill the pocket with more berries and bananas after cooking, so don't worry if it's not super pretty yet. Carefully stuff the fruit deep inside so it won't easily fall out when you flip the bread.

step 5 Brown the bread on both sides, then set it onto your serving plate. Add more berries and bananas as desired. Top with the strawberry sauce (optional; see recipe at left), maple syrup, and powdered sugar. Serve immediately.

Strawberry Sauce

step 1 Measure 1 cup of sliced strawberries into a blender or food processor. Add the powdered sugar and blend until smooth. Strain through a fine sieve or nut milk bag to remove seeds, if desired. (This step isn't necessary, but it gives the sauce a nicer mouthfeel and a more professional appearance.)

step 2 Heat the sauce in a small saucepan until simmering and slightly thickened. Remove from heat, add the extract and stir. You can make the sauce ahead of time and then warm it just before serving.

Tofu Scramble with Seitan Sausage

Tofu Scramble is one of those dishes that is just as easy to make right as it is to mess up. Making sure your tofu isn't too wet and is adequately flavored are the two main tips for scramble success.

Tofu Scramble with Seitan Sausage

Makes 3 to 4 servings

step 1 Preheat the oven to 375°F.

step 2 Prepare seitan sausage. Mix the gluten, nutritional yeast, salt, and paprika together until well combined. Mix the water, olive oil, mustard and tamari together another bowl. Add wet to dry and knead the dough for a few minutes. Let it rest for 3–5 minutes, then form the dough into a log.

step 3 Roll the log up in aluminum foil, pinching in the ends. Bake for 60 to 70 minutes. Remove and let cool.

step 4 Heat 2 tablespoons of the olive oil in a large skillet. Add the chopped broccoli and seitan and cook until the seitan is browned and the broccoli is bright green and tender-crisp. Remove from the pan and set aside.

step 5 Heat the remaining 2 tablespoons of olive oil in the pan and add the mustard and cumin seeds. When the seeds begin to pop, add the tofu to the pan and mash, allowing it to cook for a few minutes while excess water evaporates.

step 6 Once the mixture is drier, add the turmeric, beans, vinegar (or lemon juice), soy sauce, nutritional yeast, and shredded carrots. Heat through.

step 7 Add the broccoli and seitan and mix well. Season to taste with more soy sauce or vinegar as desired.

Ingredients

Seitan Sausage:

Makes approximately 4 cups

1½ cup Vital Wheat Gluten

2 tablespoons nutritional yeast

1 teaspoon salt

1 teaspoon smoked paprika

1 cup water

2 tablespoons olive oil

1 teaspoon mustard

1 tablespoon tamari or soy sauce

Tofu Mixture:

¼ cup olive oil, divided

1 head broccoli, chopped into florets

1 cup chopped, baked seitan sausage

½ teaspoon mustard seeds

½ teaspoon cumin seeds

1 block extra firm tofu, drained

½ to 1 teaspoon turmeric

¾ cup rinsed black beans

1 tablespoon white wine vinegar (or lemon juice)

3 to 4 tablespoons soy sauce

2 tablespoons nutritional yeast

½ cup shredded carrot

Weekend Pancakes Made Easy

I usually think about making pancakes sometime during the weekend, but rarely do I get around to it. I don't always want to break out my whisk and bowls and create a lot of dishes that I'll have to clean up later. One night, I had an idea: What if I made the batter the night before in my blender? One container for mixing. I could store the blender jar right in the refrigerator overnight and pour my pancakes from the blender directly into the pan the next morning. Was it as easy as I hoped? Yes, it was.

I used spelt flour, because once I realized it wasn't as scary as I thought, I figured it'd be perfect for pancakes—and it is. It's whole grain, which is always a plus, but it's much lighter and has a sweeter, milder flavor than regular whole wheat flour. Feel free to use regular flour; they'll be just as good without the spelt.

Weekend Pancakes Made Easy

Makes 2 servings

step 1 Add the soy milk to a blender, followed by the spelt flour, all-purpose flour, oil, sugar, baking powder, extract, and salt. Blend for a few seconds until combined. Scrape down any dry flour stuck to the sides and blend again. You can use the batter immediately or place the top on the blender and refrigerate overnight. If using the batter the next morning, place the blender back on the base and add 1 to 2 tablespoons of water, and then blend to mix. This thins the batter, which thickens overnight.

step 2 Preheat the oven to 200°F, or the lowest setting, and put an oven-safe plate on the middle rack.

step 3 Heat a nonstick skillet over medium heat for a few minutes, then pour the batter directly into the center of the pan. I like silver-dollar-size pancakes, 2½ inches to 3 inches in diameter, but you can make any size you want. This batter should create fairly thin pancakes.

step 4 After a few minutes of cooking, you'll see the bubbles form on the top of the pancake. The batter will start to set, and it will change color from white to dull yellow. This is when you should flip the pancakes. If your pancakes aren't brown by this time, turn the heat up a bit. If it is overly brown, turn the heat down. While cooking the pancakes, place the finished ones directly into the oven on the plate. Stack the pancakes as you go. This will keep the whole stack warm while you're cooking them.

Ingredients

1½ cups soy milk

1 cup spelt flour *(or substitute all-purpose)*

⅓ cup all-purpose flour

2 tablespoons oil

1 tablespoon sugar

1 teaspoon baking powder

1 teaspoon extract *(any flavor)*

¼ teaspoon salt

1 to 2 tablespoons water, to thin batter if needed

Earth Balance margarine, to serve

Maple syrup, to serve

step 5 While the pancakes are cooking, feel free to add blueberries, chocolate chips, or anything else you can imagine. Serve with margarine and maple syrup.

chapter two

Main Dishes

Vegan Yum Yum

Aloo Matar

ndian food isn't as complicated as you may think. I've made an effort to organize this recipe so that all the ingredients are in the order in which they are called, so that's why it looks so intense. It's really not intense. A lot of the ingredients are spices, and how hard is it to measure spices? Not hard! Once you have them, it takes two seconds to measure them. So don't freak out. It looks like a scary recipe, but it's really not.

There are a lot of spices, though. Whole spices. Do you have whole spices? I think you should. They last longer and taste better than ground spices, and you'll feel cooler using them. That being said, there are ground spices in this recipe, too. It's a perfect opportunity to go to an Indian market and look around, right?

I learned this from a wonderful Indian woman whom I only know as "Nanni," and while she's not my grandma, I wish she was. She cooks by tossing in pinches of this and spoonfuls of that, but I managed to get her to measure out most everything while we were cooking together. If you don't like spicy things, omit the chilies and chili powder, or reduce them and add the powder toward the end to suit your taste. The harder-to-find spices are marked as optional, but if you make an effort to find them, you'll be richly rewarded with a super authentic Indian meal. Really.

With this recipe, it's really worthwhile to take some time to measure out and prep everything ahead of time. Then you can just dump things in as needed and have a low-stress cooking experience. It took me about 30 minutes to leisurely prep everything and another 30ish minutes to cook. Not the fastest meal, but it's fun and tastes awesome, so it's worth it to me.

One last note: Nanni made no attempt to remove the whole spices when the dish was finished, and neither should you. Pay attention while you're eating so you don't chomp down on a bay leaf or cinnamon stick.

Aloo Matar

1/4 cup oil

Spice Batch No. 1 *(whole garam masala; see next page)*

1/2 cup finely chopped onion

1 tablespoon ginger puree *(or just finely grated ginger)*

1 tablespoon garlic puree *(or about 4 cloves of minced or pressed garlic)*

Spice Batch No. 2 *(see next page)*

1 1/2 cups diced tomatoes, blended *(fresh or canned)*

1/4 cup water

Spice Batch No. 3 *(see next page)*

2 red potatoes, peeled and chopped to 1/2-inch chunks *(2 cups or 14 ounces)*

1/4 cup cashews, ground into a powder and blended with 1/4 cup water

1 cup frozen peas

1/4 cup water, or as needed for thinning

Spice Batch No. 4 *(see next page)*

Aloo Matar

Makes 4 servings

step 1 Heat 1/4 cup oil over medium-high to high heat in a large pot that has a lid. After 2 to 3 minutes of preheating, add Spice Batch No. 1 (whole garam masala) and fry for 2 to 3 minutes, until bay leaves and cardamom change color.

step 2 Add the onion, ginger, garlic, and Spice Batch No. 2 and sauté until the onion becomes a rich golden brown.

step 3 Add the tomatoes, water, and Spice Batch No. 3; this is now a curry base for the dish. Stir, reduce heat to medium, and cook for 15 to 20 minutes loosely covered. It should be simmering, but not hard-boiling.

step 4 Meanwhile, add the potatoes to another pot that also has a lid, adding enough water to almost cover them. Bring them to a boil and place a lid loosely on top. Cook until the potatoes are fork tender, but not falling apart, about 15 to 20 minutes.

step 5 Grind cashews to a powder, then blend them in 1/4 cup water to form a milky cream. (I ground my cashews in a coffee grinder that I use for spices, and then blended them together with the water in a blender.)

step 6 Check on the curry. You know it's done when the oil begins to separate and form little pools on top of the mixture. Do not proceed until this happens. If it's not happening, stir in a little more oil and let it cook some more.

step 7 Once the oil "comes out," add cashew cream, stir well, and add the peas and drained potatoes. Mix well. If the mixture seems too thick, add up to $1/4$ cup more water.

step 8 Add Spice Batch No. 4, stir, and simmer for another 2 to 4 minutes. Serve with rice or roti (or other Indian flat bread).

Spice Batch No. 1 (whole garam masala)

2 bay leaves

$3/4$-inch cinnamon stick

6 cloves

8 green cardamom pods

Spice Batch No. 2

1 teaspoon cumin seeds

2 to 3 fresh curry leaves, finely chopped *(optional)*

1 to 2 small green chilies *(fresh, optional)*

Spice Batch No. 3

1 teaspoon turmeric

1 teaspoon coriander

$1/2$ teaspoon chili powder

1 teaspoon salt

$1/8$ teaspoon asafetida *(optional, but highly recommended)*

Spice Batch No. 4

$1/2$ teaspoon ground garam masala

$1/2$ teaspoon fenugreek leaves *(dried, optional but highly recommended)*

Broccoli Almond Sweet-and-Sour Tofu

This dish reminds me of really tasty Chinese takeout. I'm biased, though.

5/15 *Yum!!*

Broccoli Almond Sweet-and-Sour Tofu

Makes 2 servings

step 1 Slice the tofu into triangles or small cubes. Smaller is better for this recipe, since smaller pieces won't have a tendency to break up when you toss them, and they have a bigger surface-area-to-volume ratio (read: they'll be crispier).

step 2 Toss the tofu with the egg replacer/water mixture until coated. Then toss in cornstarch until each piece is coated and dry, adding more cornstarch if needed.

step 3 Heat the oil in a large nonstick skillet or wok.

step 4 While the oil is heating, make the sweet-and-sour sauce. In a small saucepan, mix rice vinegar, water, sugar, tamari, ketchup, molasses, ginger powder, and salt and whisk over medium heat until the sugar and salt is dissolved. Add the cornstarch/water mixture and whisk until the sauce thickens. If you leave the sauce unattended now, it will thicken and burn, so keep an eye on it. When thick, turn off the heat and set aside.

step 5 Place the tofu in the hot oil, being careful not to burn yourself. You don't want the tofu to be crowded or the pieces will stick to each other, so fry it in batches if needed. Fry for 3 to 5 minutes until golden on the bottom, then gently turn and brown the other side. Right before you're going to take the tofu out, add the almonds. Let them fry in the oil for 30 seconds—no longer. They should barely change color

Ingredients

1 tub extra firm tofu, pressed

2 teaspoons Ener-G Egg Replacer plus 4 teaspoons water, mixed

1/4 cup cornstarch

1/4 cup peanut or canola oil

1/2 cup sliced almonds

1 to 2 cups steamed broccoli

sesame seeds for garnish *(optional)*

Sweet-and-Sour Sauce

3 1/2 tablespoons seasoned rice vinegar

1/4 cup plus 1 tablespoon water

2 tablespoons plus 2 teaspoons sugar

2 tablespoons tamari

2 teaspoons ketchup

1 teaspoon molasses

1/4 teaspoon ginger powder

1/2 teaspoon salt

1 1/2 tablespoons cornstarch plus 2 tablespoons water, mixed

to a light golden brown.

step 6 Drain the oil from the tofu and almonds (being very careful), and place in a large bowl.

step 7 Pour the sauce on top and gently toss to completely coat. The sauce should be thick and sticky; it shouldn't pool at the bottom of the bowl.

step 8 Serve immediately with fresh steamed broccoli, adding sesame seeds on top, if using. (Alternatively, add the broccoli in with the tofu before tossing with the sweet-and-sour sauce.)

Caramelized Leek and Spaghetti Squash Polenta with White Sauce

I'm not a huge fan of onions. My mother would always tell me, "Try leeks, they're milder! You'll like them!" Last season I roasted some leeks, but I couldn't really get into them. I could see how other people would like them, but they were still too "oniony" for me. This summer we received more leeks in our community supported agriculture (CSA; where you pay a farmer at the beginning of the season to supply you with vegetables for the year) box and I decided to give it another shot.

Meanwhile, I had a spaghetti squash sitting on my counter, and I couldn't figure out what I wanted to do with it. Everyone says, "Treat it like pasta—just add sauce!!" but I've had that before. Why aren't there more creative recipes for spaghetti squash out there?

Thus, Caramelized Leek and Spaghetti Squash Polenta was born. It's kind of crazy, but it's good. And just so you know, I think it'd be good without the squash as well, so if you don't feel like buying one, just try Leek Polenta and see how you like it.

1 cup thinly sliced leeks *(2 leeks; see photos)*

1 tablespoon olive oil

1 pinch salt

1 pinch pepper

1/2 spaghetti squash, de-seeded

3 cups water

1 vegetable bouillon cube

1 cup cornmeal

cooked leeks, from above

1/2 teaspoon red pepper flakes

1/4 teaspoon salt

black pepper, to taste

White Sauce
(or make the sauce recipe given in the Hurry Up Alfredo recipe on page 196)

1/4 cup margarine

2 tablespoons all-purpose flour

1 tablespoon tahini

1 tablespoon lemon juice

1 teaspoon stone-ground mustard *(optional)*

2 tablespoons nutritional yeast

1 cup soy milk

1/2 teaspoon salt

black or white pepper, to taste

Caramelized Leek and Spaghetti Squash Polenta with White Sauce
Makes 4 to 6 servings

step 1 To prepare the leeks, trim off the roots and green leafy ends and discard these parts. Slice leeks in half lengthwise. Remove outermost layer and discard, then rinse leeks under cool water to remove sand and grit. Slice leeks crosswise into very thin slices. You should have 1 cup of packed sliced leeks.

step 2 Heat a cast-iron (preferable) or large sauté pan over medium heat. Add the leeks, oil, salt, and pepper. Stirring occasionally, cook leeks for at least 5 minutes or until partly caramelized (brown and soft). Leeks should taste sweet and almost buttery with a mild onion aftertaste (not raw, sharp, or bitter) when finished.

step 3 Remove to a bowl and set aside.

Vegan Yum Yum

Squash Preparation Options:

To prepare the squash, you may microwave, boil, or bake it (instructions follow below for all methods. You will be cooking the squash while preparing the polenta).

If microwaving the squash (the fastest method):

step 1 Halve the squash widthwise. This is a winter squash and it's hard enough to cut as it is—most sources will tell you to cut the squash lengthwise, but widthwise is easier (and therefore safer since you don't need your knife slipping when exerting a lot of pressure on it), and it will fit into your microwave better. Remove seeds from squash and discard them.

step 2 Place the squash in a bowl, cut side down, and fill with water until 1 inch of the bottom of the squash is covered. Cover loosely with plastic wrap and microwave for 12 minutes on high, letting it stand for another 5 minutes in the microwave before removing.

step 3 *Carefully* remove the squash, dump the water, and cut the squash into quarters (this shortens the strings so the polenta will be easier to stir and cut).

step 4 When cool enough to handle, use a fork to scrape the spaghetti-like strands into a bowl and set aside. You should have 2 cups squash, packed. If the squash seems wet, roll it in a paper towel and then in a tea/terry cloth towel and squeeze it to dry it out, as you don't want to add a lot of moisture to the polenta.

If boiling the squash (the easiest method):

step 1 Prick the squash with a fork several times, put it into a very large pot, fill with water, and begin heating on the stove. Boil the squash for 20 minutes until just tender; it doesn't need to be super soft. Drain, cut the squash in half, and remove the seeds.

step 2 Cut one of the halves into quarters (this shortens the strings so the polenta will be easier to stir and cut), then scrape the strands out with a fork. You should have 2 cups squash, packed. If the squash seems wet, roll it in a paper towel and then in a tea/terry cloth towel and squeeze it to dry it out, as you don't want to add a lot of moisture to the polenta.

If baking the squash:

step 1 Preheat the oven to 375°F.

step 2 Cut the squash in half and scrape out the seeds. Place cut side down on a baking sheet covered with oiled tinfoil. Bake for 30 to 40 minutes or until tender.

step 3 Cut one of the halves into quarters (this shortens the strings so the polenta will be easier to stir and cut), then scrape the strands out with a fork. You should have 2 cups of squash, packed. If the squash seems wet, roll it in a paper towel and then in a tea/terry cloth towel and squeeze it to dry it out, as you don't want to add a lot of moisture to the polenta.

Preparing the Polenta:

step 1 While the squash is cooking, add the bouillon cube to 3 cups of water and bring to a boil.

step 2 Add the cornmeal in a steady stream, whisking thoroughly. Continue to whisk.

step 3 Add leeks, pepper flakes, salt, and pepper and cook over medium-low heat for 20 minutes or so.

step 4 When the squash is ready, add it to the polenta (you might want to switch to a wooden spoon to stir, since the whisk is probably more trouble than it's worth due to the thickness of the polenta). Mix well and cook for an additional 5 minutes, being careful not to burn.

step 5 Scrape out the polenta into an oiled 8-x-8-inch brownie pan (or something of similar size), cover with plastic wrap, and refrigerate for at least 1 hour until set.

step 6 To make the white sauce, whisk the margarine in a saucepan over medium-low heat until melted. Add the flour and whisk into a paste. Add the tahini, lemon juice, mustard, and yeast and whisk well. Slowly add soy milk, whisking well to make a smooth sauce.

Add salt and pepper and whisk over medium-high heat until mixture is thickened; it should coat the back of a spoon thickly.

step 7 To serve the polenta, you may grill, sauté, or broil it as desired. If you choose to sauté it (the photo above shows sautéed polenta), make sure your pan is quite hot, otherwise the oil will seep into your polenta and make it taste gross. Serve with the white sauce on top.

Creamy Broccoli Mushroom Bake

So, this is an ugly duckling. It was hard to get it to look as good as it does, but it's still no beauty pageant winner. However, what it lacks in looks it makes up for in soothing, creamy, comfort food awesomeness. It's sort of a variation on baked mac and cheese. The sauce base is a slightly tweaked version of the sauce used in the Hurry Up Alfredo recipe on page 196, so if you like that sauce (and broccoli and mushrooms), you'll like this.

I use orzo pasta because it's quick cooking and small enough to help the casserole stay in a block when you cut it. You can use any smallish pasta shape you want, but you might have to make more than 1 cup depending on what size the shape is.

Creamy Broccoli Mushroom Bake

Makes 4 to 5 servings

step 1 To make the Alfredo sauce, mix the soy milk, margarine, soy sauce, tahini, lemon juice, nutritional yeast, cashews, cornstarch, mustard, and garlic in a blender until it is as smooth as possible, then set aside.

step 2 Begin boiling water for the pasta and add when ready.

step 3 Preheat the oven to 400°F.

step 4 Separate the florets from the stem of the broccoli. Chop stem into smallish pieces and place in the work bowl of a food processor. Pulse a few times to break it down some more. Add the florets and pulse until the entire mixture is fairly fine, though some chunks of broccoli are fine (and even desired). Remove from the food processor; you should have 2½ cups.

step 5 Process the mushrooms until uniform, remove from food processor, and add to the broccoli. You should have ½ cup of mushrooms.

step 6 Heat a bit of olive oil in a large skillet. Add the onions and sauté until softened and beginning to color. Then add the broccoli/mushroom mixture and salt and sauté until the mixture cooks down slightly and everything has softened, about 5 to 7 minutes. Turn off the heat.

step 7 Drain the pasta when done. Add it to the

Hurry Up Alfredo Sauce, Tweaked

1 cup soy milk

2 tablespoons Earth Balance margarine *(or vegetable oil with a small pinch of salt)*

2 tablespoons soy sauce

2 tablespoons tahini

1 tablespoon fresh lemon juice

¼ cup nutritional yeast

¼ cup raw, unsalted cashews

2 tablespoons cornstarch

2 teaspoons Dijon mustard

2 to 4 garlic cloves *(optional)*

1 cup orzo

1 stalk broccoli, 2½ cups after processing

1 cup mushrooms *(button, portabella, or cremini)*, ½ cup after processing

2 to 3 tablespoons olive oil

½ cup finely chopped onion

¼ to ½ cup bread crumbs, for topping

1 pinch salt

½ teaspoon smoked paprika

black pepper, to taste

1 green or red bell pepper, for garnish *(optional)*

broccoli/mushroom mixture and then pour the Alfredo sauce over it and mix well. Taste and add more salt at this point if desired. Scrape out the mixture into a lightly oiled (important!) medium-size casserole dish. Top with bread crumbs and sprinkle with a drizzle of olive oil, salt, paprika, and pepper. Cover tightly in foil and bake for 25 minutes.

step 8 Remove the foil and bake for an extra 5 minutes to brown the top. Let it rest for 10 minutes before serving.

Serving Suggestions: I like to serve this topped with fresh, finely diced green pepper on top. It gives a nice, crunchy, sweet pop to the soft, creamy casserole. Plus, it makes it look better. I also dust with more paprika. While this recipe keeps well, it becomes a little dry the next day, so add a splash of soy milk when reheating. It's also good with ketchup, if you're into that sort of thing.

READER/CUSTOMER CARE SURVEY

We care about your opinions! Please take a moment to fill out our online Reader Survey at **http://survey.hcibooks.com.**
As a **"THANK YOU"** you will receive a **VALUABLE INSTANT COUPON** towards future book purchases
as well as a **SPECIAL GIFT** available only online! Or, you may mail this card back to us.

(PLEASE PRINT IN ALL CAPS)

First Name _____ MI. ___ Last Name _____

Address _____ City _____

State _____ Zip _____ Email _____

1. Gender
❑ Female   ❑ Male

2. Age
❑ 8 or younger
❑ 9-12   ❑ 13-16
❑ 17-20   ❑ 21-30
❑ 31+

3. Did you receive this book as a gift?
❑ Yes   ❑ No

4. Annual Household Income
❑ under $25,000
❑ $25,000 - $34,999
❑ $35,000 - $49,999
❑ $50,000 - $74,999
❑ over $75,000

5. What are the ages of the children living in your house?
❑ 0 - 14   ❑ 15+

6. Marital Status
❑ Single
❑ Married
❑ Divorced
❑ Widowed

7. How did you find out about the book?
(please choose one)
❑ Recommendation
❑ Store Display
❑ Online
❑ Catalog/Mailing
❑ Interview/Review

8. Where do you usually buy books?
(please choose one)
❑ Bookstore
❑ Online
❑ Book Club/Mail Order
❑ Price Club (Sam's Club, Costco's, etc.)
❑ Retail Store (Target, Wal-Mart, etc.)

9. What subject do you enjoy reading about the most?
(please choose one)
❑ Parenting/Family
❑ Relationships
❑ Recovery/Addictions
❑ Health/Nutrition
❑ Christianity
❑ Spirituality/Inspiration
❑ Business Self-help
❑ Women's Issues
❑ Sports

10. What attracts you most to a book?
(please choose one)
❑ Title
❑ Cover Design
❑ Author
❑ Content

TAPE IN MIDDLE; DO NOT STAPLE

BUSINESS REPLY MAIL

FIRST-CLASS MAIL PERMIT NO 45 DEERFIELD BEACH, FL

POSTAGE WILL BE PAID BY ADDRESSEE

Health Communications, Inc.
3201 SW 15th Street
Deerfield Beach FL 33442-9875

FOLD HERE

Comments

Creamy Sweet Potato Bake

I love the versatility of my Alfredo sauce. It's my go-to creamy sauce, and it goes wonderfully in this dish with tender sweet potatoes, dark kale, and some nutmeg, ginger, and thyme to bring the dish together. It's really easy to cook, but it makes a satisfying meal.

3 cups fusilli pasta *(or other similar shape)*

1 head kale, deveined and chopped

1½ pounds sweet potatoes

Alfredo Sauce

1¼ cups soy milk

⅓ cup raw, unsalted cashews

⅓ cup nutritional yeast

3 tablespoons low-sodium tamari

2 tablespoons Earth Balance margarine

1 tablespoon tahini

1 tablespoon lemon juice

½ teaspoon Dijon mustard

¼ teaspoon powdered ginger

1 pinch nutmeg

¾ teaspoon dried thyme

½ teaspoon paprika, sweet or smoked *(optional)*

black pepper, to taste

Bread crumbs, for topping *(optional)*

Creamy Sweet Potato Bake

Makes 3 to 4 servings

step 1 Bring a large pot of salted water to a boil, then add the pasta.

step 2 Two or three minutes before the pasta is completely cooked, add the chopped kale to the boiling water. When pasta is cooked and the kale is bright green but tender, drain and set aside.

step 3 Chop the sweet potatoes into bite-size chunks. Boil in salted water until tender, but not falling apart. Drain.

step 4 Preheat the oven to 400°F.

step 5 To make the Alfredo sauce, blend the soy milk, cashews, nutritional yeast, tamari, margarine, tahini, lemon juice, mustard, ginger, nutmeg, thyme, paprika, and black pepper in a blender. Blend well for several minutes until the sauce is smooth and creamy. Taste and season, if necessary.

step 6 Combine the pasta, kale, and the sweet potatoes with the sauce and stir well. Place in a casserole dish and top with bread crumbs, if desired. Bake for 20 minutes or until hot and bubbly. Serve.

I made this dish after going out for Indian food with my best friend Sandy and seeing her order it every single time. I started to get jealous, because I could never taste her dish due to the cream. So here's my vegan version: a rich, creamy, filling lentil dish that's perfect for cold winter nights. Or any night. (Especially if you're Sandy.)

1 cup masoor dal *(substitute French or green lentils)*

2 cups water

¼ cup oil

½ cup chopped onion

2 cloves

1 1-inch piece of cinnamon stick

1 bay leaf

2 green cardamom pods

1 x 1-inch piece of fresh ginger, peeled and minced

1 clove garlic, minced

1¼ cups tomatoes, diced

½ teaspoon salt

½ cup water *(optional)*

⅔ cup cashews

⅔ cup water

Dal Makhni

Makes 2 to 3 servings

step 1 Cook the lentils in 2 cups water until tender, about 40 minutes.

step 2 Heat the oil in a large skillet. Add the onion and cook until caramelized and reddish brown, being careful not to burn.

step 3 Add the cloves, cinnamon stick, bay leaf, and cardamom pods and fry for 2 to 3 minutes.

step 4 Add the ginger and garlic and cook an additional 2 minutes.

step 5 Add the tomatoes and salt and cook until slightly reduced, about 5 minutes.

step 6 Stir in the lentils and additional water, if needed, to thin.

step 7 Blend the cashews in a blender, slowly adding the water until it's all combined and a rich cream forms. Stir this cream into the lentils as desired, saving some for presentation when serving. Serve, garnishing with a drizzle of cashew cream.

Delicata Squash Stuffed with Cherry Apple Almond Couscous

This is a really flexible dish. It takes just about 30 minutes to make, which is awesome, because it seems like it would take longer. This is great as a fancy side dish (1 squash half per person) or a main dish (2 per person) if you serve something like sautéed greens or a salad on the side. Crispy kale goes great with this!

This is also a wonderful dish to make for the holidays. It makes enough side dishes for 8 people and it goes well with other holiday foods. It's also low-fat (hooray!), so it's one less dish on the holiday table that will end up on your butt.

Delicata squash is one of my favorites because it's sweet, beautiful, and quick cooking. And they're not a pain to cut in half, so they get major bonus points for that. If you need to substitute, look for butternut, acorn, or carnival squash, or any sweet squash you fancy.

4 Delicata squashes, about 5 to 6 inches long *(or other similar-size sweet squash)*

olive oil to oil cookie sheet

salt

1³/₄ cups water

1 cup dried cherries

³/₄ teaspoon salt

1 Granny Smith apple

¹/₃ cup sliced almonds

1 teaspoon Earth Balance margarine *(optional)*

1 cup couscous

3 tablespoons agave nectar

3 tablespoons mustard *(stone-ground or Dijon style)*

¹/₄ teaspoon plus 1 pinch salt

Delicata Squash Stuffed with Cherry Apple Almond Couscous

Makes 8 side dishes or 4 main dishes*

(*Note: The couscous is nice on its own, so feel free to make less squash if you don't mind having some couscous left over for another meal.)

step 1   Preheat the oven to 400°F.

step 2   Halve the squashes lengthwise. Scoop out the seeds with a spoon and discard. Sprinkle lightly with salt, then place cut side down on a lightly oiled cookie sheet (I use a Silpat baking mat, but parchment paper or foil will work to minimize mess). Bake squashes for 30 minutes.

step 3   Meanwhile, place the water, cherries, and salt in a pot that has a tight-fitting lid. Bring the cherries to a boil, then turn off the heat.

step 4   Dice the apple into approximately ¹/₄-inch chunks. Add the apples and almonds to the cherries and let stand for 5 minutes, until cherries are plumped and apples are softened.

Strain out cherries, apples, and almonds and place them in a large bowl, reserving the liquid. The liquid should be reddish and equal to 1¹/₄ cup now. If not, adjust by pouring some off or adding water.

step 5   Add the liquid back to the pot and bring to a boil. Add margarine, if using. When the liquid boils, pour in the couscous, give the pot a little shake, cover, and turn off the heat. Let stand for 10 minutes or until you're ready to stuff.

Vegan Yum Yum

step 6 During the last 10 minutes, make the dressing by mixing together the agave nectar, mustard, and salt. Clear a space to fill the squashes. (When I got to this step, there were 10 minutes left on the squash.)

step 7 Remove the squash from the oven and carefully use a spatula to take them off your baking sheet. The squash should be very soft, so take care not to smoosh or rip them. It's prettier to fill them and then place them on your serving dish, because you will get couscous everywhere while filling.

step 8 Fluff the couscous with a fork, then place it in the bowl that has the apple/cherry/almond mixture and combine well.

step 9 Mix half of the dressing into the couscous and spoon the mixture into the squash cavities. Plate the squashes, then drizzle the remaining dressing over the top, if desired.

Garnish with extra dried cherries and almonds and serve immediately.

Italian Rice and Beans

I love the way this dish turns out. I especially love the lemon zest on top. It really does something magical. But I must warn you, I think a Microplane grater is absolutely necessary. A friend of mine bought me one as a present, and my word, it makes the finest, lightest, fluffiest zest I've ever had. It practically melts in your mouth.

Italian Rice and Beans

Makes 2 to 3 servings

step 1 Start cooking the rice (while I use a rice cooker, you can also boil it on the stove top according to package instructions).

step 2 When rice is finished, heat the olive oil in a sauté pan over medium heat.

step 3 Add the herbs, tomatoes, and pine nuts. When the pine nuts start to turn golden brown, add the beans. Toss gently, trying your best to keep the beans whole.

step 4 Add the salt and vinegar and stir gently. Turn down the heat to low.

step 5 Place spinach in one layer on top of the beans. Place the hot, steaming rice over the spinach and leave for 30 seconds or so, until you see the spinach start to wilt. Mix gently and taste. If it doesn't have the "pop" that you want, add in a little bit more vinegar and salt to taste.

step 6 Grate the lemon zest on top of the rice and beans and serve.

Ingredients

1 cup brown rice, uncooked

3 tablespoons of olive oil

2 to 3 teaspoons Italian herbs of your choice *(basil, oregano, marjoram, rosemary, etc.)*

$1/2$ cup oil-packed sun-dried tomatoes, sliced into strips

$1/4$ cup pine nuts

1 can great northern beans, rinsed and drained

$1/2$ teaspoon kosher salt

2 teaspoons balsamic vinegar

2 large handfuls of baby spinach

Zest from 1 lemon

Marmalade Tofu with Kale and Lemon Pearl Couscous

Marmalade chicken is one of those simple dinner dishes that home cooks have been preparing for themselves or their families for years because it's not only easy, but also tasty.

This dish is as easy as you want it to be, super flavorful, and infinitely customizable. You can use a base of rice, couscous, pasta, quinoa, millet, polenta (and so on) and dress it up with any simply prepared greens or veggies you've got.

I grilled the tofu after I baked it because I love grill marks. The use of a grill or a grill pan is totally optional, unless you're like me and like really pretty tofu. If you're free of my strange tofu vanity issues, don't worry one bit. However, if you do break out the grill pan, be careful not to burn the 'fu. All the sugar in the marmalade makes for easily scorched tofu if you're not careful. I may or may not be speaking from experience (cough cough).

Marmalade Tofu with Kale and Lemon Pearl Couscous

Makes 2 servings with leftover tofu *(recipe doubles well)*

step 1 Preheat the oven to 400°F.

step 2 Cut the pressed tofu into 8 even rectangles. Oil a baking dish that will fit all of the tofu snuggly.

step 3 Make the marmalade marinade by whisking together the marmalade, tamari, lemon juice, chili flakes, pepper, and ginger (if using). Place the tofu pieces in the baking dish and cover with marinade.

step 4 Bake the tofu for 30 minutes, flipping halfway through. There should still be a little marinade in the bottom of the dish after baking—just enough to use as a glaze.

step 5 When the tofu is halfway done, heat 2 teaspoons of the oil in a large skillet and add dry couscous. Stir for a few minutes until each pearl is coated and lightly toasted. Add the lemon juice, lemon zest, and salt. Add 2 cups of the water and let simmer, stir-

Ingredients

1 14-ounce block of extra-firm tofu, well pressed *(or 4 seitan cutlets; see page 117)*

1 recipe of Marmalade Marinade *(see recipe below)*

4 teaspoons vegetable oil, split into two portions

1 cup pearl couscous

2 teaspoons fresh lemon juice

Zest from 1 lemon

$1/2$ (scant) teaspoon salt

2 to $2^{1}/2$ cups water

1 bunch kale *(or approximately 2 cups vegetables of your choice)*

2 tablespoons water

$1/4$ cup sliced almonds

1 to 2 teaspoons tamari

Marmalade Marinade

$1/4$ cup and 1 tablespoon marmalade

2 tablespoons reduced-sodium tamari or soy sauce

1 tablespoon fresh lemon juice

$1/2$ teaspoon hot chili flakes *(optional)*

Black pepper, fresh ground

$1/4$ teaspoon ginger *(optional)*

ring frequently, and watch as the couscous absorbs the liquid. When all the liquid is absorbed, try a pearl to see if it is cooked through. Add more water if necessary. (Alternatively, you can also boil the couscous, drain, and then mix in the salt, juice, and zest with a little oil.)

step 6 In the last few minutes, heat the remaining 2 teaspoons of oil in a wok or large skillet. (The tofu will hold nicely in a warm oven if you need more time.) Add the washed and torn kale and toss to coat. Add the water to the hot pan and quickly cover with any lid that will fit to quick-steam the kale. Remove the lid after a few minutes (admire how tender and green the kale looks) and sauté to cook off any remaining liquid.

step 7 Add almonds and tamari, stirring well, until the almonds are lightly toasted.

step 8 Plate the couscous and then the kale. Add the tofu on top and drizzle any remaining glaze over everything. Garnish with extra almonds if desired.

Pineapple Baked Tofu with Seared Pineapple Rings and Nutty Greens

I came up with this recipe a week before my husband and I took our honeymoon to Belize, when I had coconuts and pineapple on my mind. It uses both canned coconut milk and canned pineapple rings, so you don't have to live on a tropical island to make it.

1 block extra firm tofu, pressed and sliced into 8 rectangles

³/₄ cup pineapple juice *(from the can of pineapple rings)*

¹/₄ cup tamari

1 tablespoon seasoned rice vinegar

3 tablespoons peanut oil, split into 1 tablespoon and 2 tablespoons

1 teaspoon Old Bay Seasoning, split into two ¹/₂-teaspoon amounts

1¹/₂ cups brown rice cooked in 3 cups water

8 pineapple rings

2 large bunches spinach, kale, collards, or your favorite greens, washed and chopped

¹/₄ cup crushed peanuts, almonds, or cashews

Leftover marinade from the tofu *(¹/₃ cup liquid)*

¹/₄ cup coconut milk

1 tablespoon cornstarch mixed with 1 tablespoon water

Pineapple Baked Tofu with Seared Pineapple Rings and Nutty Greens

Makes 4 servings

step 1 Preheat oven to 400°F.

step 2 To make the pineapple marinade, mix the pineapple juice, tamari, rice vinegar, peanut oil, and ¹/₂ teaspoon of the Old Bay Seasoning in an 8 x 8-inch baking dish (or whatever works). Place the tofu in the marinade so it just covers the slices. Bake for 20 minutes, flipping over after 10 minutes.

step 3 After you put the tofu in the oven, put the rice on to cook. As it's cooking, prepare the pineapple rings. Lightly oil a very hot wok or skillet and sear the rings, both sides, until nicely colored. Set aside until ready to serve.

step 4 Remove the tofu from the baking dish and place it on a baking sheet covered with parchment paper, reserving the marinade from the baking dish. Increase the oven temperature to 425°F and bake for another 20 minutes, flipping over after 10 minutes.

step 5 Heat the greens in the same wok that the pineapple rings were seared in, with just enough oil to coat. Stir-fry (tongs help) until the greens are tender. Add the crushed nuts and mix well.

step 6 Place the leftover marinade into a skillet or saucepan and heat over medium heat until simmering. Add the coconut milk and mix with a whisk.

Turn off the heat, add the cornstarch/water mixture and whisk until thickened. Plate the rice, greens, tofu and pineapple. Spoon the sauce over the finished dish.

Rainbow Rice and Beans

'm sure this recipe started out as normal rice and beans. Over the years it has morphed into a shameless display of all the vegetables we keep in stock at all times.

I love this meal because it's really easy, very comforting, and full of all sorts of good-for-me things. It's also very flexible in terms of what vegetables you can add. I've used broccoli and mushrooms in the past, but I'm sure anything from kale to bell peppers would work just fine. The more you add, the more fun and colorful the dish becomes.

Rainbow Rice and Beans

Makes 2 huge servings (doubles nicely)

step 1 Start the rice with two cups of cold water or whatever ratio of water to rice works best for the type of rice you are using.

step 2 When the rice is almost done cooking, heat the vegetable oil in a large skillet. If using onion, add it and cook until golden brown.

step 3 Add the cumin, cumin seeds (if using), coriander, red pepper flakes, oregano, and mustard seeds (if using), and sauté until the spices begin to bubble up a little bit, being careful not to burn them (I don't need to tell you that, right?). If you're using mustard seeds, they'll start popping and jumping out of the pan—just warning you.

step 4 Add the beans, tamari (or soy sauce), and the vegan Worcestershire sauce and simmer on low, covered, until the rice is done.

step 5 Add the peas, carrots, and corn for a few moments until defrosted.

step 6 Add the rice to the pan, stirring well to mix in the beans and the veggies and to coat with sauce. If you want to make it "richer," stir in a knob of margarine at the end. Serve immediately.

Ingredients

1 cup brown basmati rice, dry *(or white rice if you're in a rush)*

1 tablespoon of vegetable oil

1/4 cup chopped onion *(optional)*

1/2 teaspoon cumin, crushed

1/2 teaspoon cumin seeds *(optional)*

1/2 teaspoon coriander

1/2 teaspoon red pepper flakes

1/2 teaspoon oregano

1/2 teaspoon mustard seeds *(optional)*

1 can black beans, partially drained

3 tablespoons tamari *(or soy sauce)*

3 tablespoons vegan Worcestershire sauce *(see recipe on page 278)*

1/2 cup frozen peas

2 medium carrots, shredded

1/2 cup frozen corn

Earth Balance margarine *(optional)*

love this casserole. It has three layers: an herb tofu layer on the bottom, steamed cauliflower mixed with a creamy, cheezy white sauce in the middle, and a yummy tomato sauce on top, hence the name.

The white sauce will work well for a variety of other recipes. Consider it for anything where you want a mild but rich sauce as a complement. It's also great on top of asparagus, steamed broccoli, or on baked potatoes.

Red and White Cauliflower Bake

Makes 4 servings

step 1 Start by making the marinara. Heat the margarine or olive oil in a sauté pan over medium heat. Once hot, add the herbs and sauté for a minute or two, being careful not to burn. Add garlic and sauté for 30 seconds. Add tomatoes and bouillon or salt. Simmer until the sauce is the consistency you like; about 10 minutes works for me. Since this sauce is going on top of a casserole, you might want to cook it a bit longer than you usually would, so that it's not watery; a thicker sauce will work best here.

step 2 While the sauce is cooking, chop the cauliflower into very small pieces and steam.

step 3 Then make the herbed tofu ricotta. Mix together the tofu, salt, basil, rosemary, marjoram, lemon juice, yeast, olive oil (if using), pepper, and the cornstarch/water mixture.

step 4 Next, make the white sauce. Whisk the margarine in a saucepan over medium-low heat until melted. Add the flour and whisk into a paste. Add the tahini, lemon juice, mustard, and the yeast and whisk well. Slowly add the soy milk, whisking well to make a smooth sauce. Add the salt and pepper and whisk over medium-high heat until mixture is thickened; it should coat the back of a spoon thickly.

Ingredients

Simple Marinara

1 tablespoon vegan margarine or olive oil

2 teaspoons dried Italian herbs *(my favorites are basil, marjoram, and oregano)*

2 to 4 cloves garlic, minced

1 can *(14.5 ounces)* stewed tomatoes, blended

1/2 vegetable bouillon cube or 1/2 teaspoon plus salt

4 cups cauliflower, chopped small and steamed

Herbed Tofu Ricotta

1 package extra-firm tofu, well pressed and crumbled

1/2 to 3/4 teaspoon salt

2 teaspoons dried basil

1 teaspoon dried rosemary

1 teaspoon dried marjoram

1 tablespoon lemon juice

2 tablespoons nutritional yeast

1 tablespoon olive oil *(optional)*

Fresh cracked black pepper, to taste

(Ingredients continued on next page)

2 tablespoons cornstarch mixed with 2 tablespoons water *(this helps it set up in the bottom of the pan; omit this for other uses of this ricotta recipe)*

White Sauce

¼ cup Earth Balance margarine

¼ cup all-purpose flour

1 tablespoon tahini

1 tablespoon lemon juice

1 teaspoon stone-ground mustard

2 tablespoons nutritional yeast

1 cup soy milk

½ teaspoon salt

Black or white pepper, to taste

1 cup bread crumbs

To Assemble the Casserole:

step 1 Place the tofu ricotta in an oiled 1½-quart casserole dish—shallow and long works better than deep and narrow. Press it down to form an even layer.

step 2 Mix the cauliflower with the white sauce and spread it over the tofu in an even layer. Add the tomatoe sauce on top of the cauliflower, top with bread crumbs, and bake at 400°F for 20 to 25 minutes until bubbly and browned.

step 3 Let stand at least 5 to 10 minutes before serving so the casserole can set up. It is a "soft set" while warm, though, so be gentle if you want identifiable squares. It tastes just as good all mushed up, though. This reheats really well and holds its shape better the second time around.

These burgers are really fast to throw together, and you can play with your own spice mix or add-ins if you want.

Ingredients

1 cup seitan

1 14-ounce can black beans, rinsed and drained

1 tablespoon vegan Worcestershire sauce *(see recipe on page 278)*

1 tablespoon tamari or soy sauce

½ to 1 cup bread crumbs *(or 2 slices of bread, toasted)* *

2 tablespoons all-purpose flour

½ cup frozen corn

½ teaspoon smoked paprika

½ teaspoon cumin

½ teaspoon chili powder

¼ teaspoon celery salt *(replace with salt or mushroom stock powder if you don't care for it)*

2 tablespoons high-heat vegetable oil for pan frying

*Note: You may need to adjust the amount of bread crumbs depending on how moist the seitan is. Seitan varies a lot in moisture content. I use a wet seitan, so 1 cup of bread crumbs is on the upper limit of what you may need. Start with ½ cup and add more until the burgers are firm enough but still moist enough to stick together.

Seitan Black Bean Corn Burgers

Makes 10 servings

step 1 If the seitan is packed in water or broth, drain it. Add it to a food processor and process until finely chopped (a few remaining bigger chunks are okay).

step 2 Add the beans and process until finely chopped (you may still see the occasional bean piece). Remove this mixture to a mixing bowl.

step 3 Add the vegan Worcestershire sauce, tamari, bread crumbs, flour, corn, paprika, cumin, chili powder, and celery salt to the seitan/bean mixture and mix well with your hands (you can also use a spoon, but hands work best!). Adjust the mixture with salt, to taste, or add more bread crumbs if the mixture is too wet. It should be moist, but not gloppy. For example, if you stuff your ¼-cup measure with it, you should have to pry it out. If it glops out by itself, it's probably too wet.

step 4 Heat the oil in a pan over medium-high heat, preferably cast iron.

step 5 Begin forming patties (¼ cup of mixture per patty works well). My patties were about the size of my palm and fairly thin to avoid a too-mushy center. You can form all of the patties ahead of time and place them on wax/parchment paper, foil, plastic wrap, or whatever. Use the wax paper to help you remove the patties without mushing them.

step 6 Fry patties four at a time, or however many will

reasonably fit into the pan (leaving room for flipping) until dark brown on either side. If you let them burn (just a little) it will taste more like a grilled burger. Serve immediately.

Soy-Mirin Tofu with Snow Peas and Peanut Sauce

This recipe is another one of my favorites. It makes a great larger lunch or a filling dinner. It's also easy to scale. For every two people eating, you will need 1 block of tofu, 1 glaze recipe, 1 peanut sauce recipe, 2 cups of veggies (snow peas), and 1 carrot. If you're making it for a crowd and you have to cook the tofu in batches, keep it warm in a low oven until you've pan-fried all that's needed.

You can definitely use water instead of coconut milk in this recipe. I only use coconut milk when I happen to have an open can in the fridge. Broccoli works really well in this dish if you can't find snow peas. Steam the broccoli as opposed to blanching.

Vegan Yum Yum

Soy-Mirin Tofu with Snow Peas and Peanut Sauce

Makes 2 servings

step 1 Start cooking the rice in 2 cups water, in a rice cooker or on the stove. To make the peanut sauce, mix the peanut butter, coconut milk (or water), sugar, soy sauce, rice vinegar, powdered ginger, and hot chili oil (if using) until smooth (be patient, it might take a moment to smooth out) and set aside. If you're using coconut milk, you may need to add an additional 1 tablespoon of water to get it thin enough.

step 2 While the rice is cooking, press the tofu.

step 3 Trim the snow peas, blanch them in salted boiling water for 1 minute, drain, shock in a bowl of ice-cold water, and then set aside.

step 4 Shred the carrot, set aside.

step 5 Mix together the soy sauce and mirin for the soy-mirin glaze. When the rice is nearly done (or completely done) begin cooking the tofu.

step 6 Pan-fry the tofu in the oil over high heat in a 10-inch cast-iron or nonstick skillet until browned on at least two sides of every cube. (If you use nonstick or cast iron, only 1 tablespoon or less of oil should be needed, and you won't have to drain off any oil.) Turn off the heat.

step 7 Add the snow peas and pour the soy-mirin mixture over the tofu and peas, mixing well. It will bubble up and form a light glaze.

step 8 Plate the rice, tofu and peas, carrot, and crushed peanuts. Drizzle with sauce and serve.

Main Dishes

Ingredients

1 cup dry brown rice

2 cups water

1/4 cup peanut butter

1/4 cup coconut milk or water

1 tablespoon sugar

1 tablespoon soy sauce

1 tablespoon seasoned rice vinegar

1/4 teaspoon powdered ginger

1 teaspoon hot chili oil (optional)

1 block extra firm tofu, pressed and cut into small squares

2 cups snow peas, trimmed, cut into 2-inch pieces and blanched with pinch of salt

1 carrot, peeled and shredded

1 tablespoon soy sauce

1 tablespoon mirin

1 tablespoon canola or peanut oil for pan frying

Crushed peanuts as garnish (optional)

Sweet Chili Lime Tofu

I've been thinking recently about the five flavors that many Thai dishes revolve around: hot, sweet, salty, sour, and bitter. I wasn't necessarily looking to create a Thai dish, but a dish that balances those five flavors without being overly complicated. I'm really pleased with the result: tofu so easy to prepare you won't mind whipping it up after work. And this recipe has no added fat! It certainly has a good deal of sugar and salt, but hey, old habits die hard.

If you've read my blog for any length of time, you'll probably realize that this recipe falls within the basic equation for my favorite meals: flavorful tofu + dark leafy green + grain/rice/pasta base. I love this combination because it's easy and super customizable, depending on what you have on hand. I use collard greens and quinoa in this recipe, but feel free to use spinach, kale, mustard greens, chard, arugula, Chinese broccoli, cabbage, or whatever for the greens, and wheat pasta, rice, millet, rice noodles, barley, orzo, and so on instead of the quinoa. Just keep in mind that if you use brown rice, you'll need to adjust the amount of water to 1 cup.

Vegan Yum Yum

Sweet Chili Lime Tofu

Makes 2 to 3 servings

step 1 Combine the quinoa, lime zest, cardamom, cinnamon, salt, and water in a pot with a tight-fitting lid. Bring to a boil, then cover and reduce heat to low. Cook for 20 minutes, then turn off heat. Do not open the lid. Let it steam for 10 minutes before serving.

step 2 Prepare the sweet chili lime sauce by whisking together the sugar, tamari, lime juice, lime zest, red chili flakes, garlic, salt, and mint until the sugar and salt is dissolved. Set aside.

step 3 Drain the tofu and cut it into small triangles. I slice the block into 8 rectangles, then each rectangle in half to make 2 squares per rectangle. I cut each square diagonally to make 4 triangles per square. Tofu geometry is my favorite kind of math! You can cut the tofu however you please, but a thinner, smaller shape will work best for this method.

³/₄ cup quinoa, rubbed/rinsed in cool water and drained

Zest from 1 lime, separated into two equal parts

2 bruised cardamom pods *(optional)*

1 tiny stick of cinnamon *(a broken piece of a larger stick) (optional)*

¹/₄ teaspoon salt

1¹/₃ cups water

Sweet Chili Lime Sauce *(see recipe below)*

1 14-ounce block of extra-firm tofu

1 bunch collard greens, washed with middle veins removed

2 to 3 tablespoons water

1 teaspoon lime juice

1 pinch salt

Lime slices, for garnish *(optional)*

Mint leaves, for garnish *(optional)*

Sweet Chili Lime Sauce

3 tablespoons sugar

3 tablespoons reduced-sodium tamari or soy sauce

1³/₄ tablespoons fresh lime juice

¹/₂ zest of the lime

¹/₂ teaspoon red chili flakes *(or 1 to 2 fresh hot chilies, minced)*

1 clove garlic, pressed *(optional)*

¹/₄ teaspoon salt

4 mint leaves, chiffonade *(stack the leaves, roll them up, and slice thinly)*

step 4 Heat a well-seasoned cast-iron or nonstick skillet over medium heat. A 10-inch skillet will fit all the tofu, so if you're using a smaller skillet, you'll need to do this in batches. In order to properly "dry fry" the tofu, you'll need a pan the tofu won't stick to even without any oil.

step 5 Spread the tofu out in one layer in the pan. Using a spatula, press the tofu. The liquid will squeeze out and boil away, and the tofu will begin to turn golden. The more water that evaporates, the sturdier the tofu will be, so be gentle at first to prevent the tofu from breaking up. After several minutes, flip the tofu over and press the other side. After about 10 minutes of dry frying, you can turn off the heat and set the tofu aside for finishing later or proceed by adding the sauce. (You might want to set the tofu aside before finishing in order to prepare the collards, below.)

step 6 To finish the tofu, bring the pan back up to temperature if it's not already very hot. You want to heat the pan and the tofu over high heat, making sure the tofu is hot all the way through. Add the chili lime sauce and stir to coat the tofu. Turn off the heat. The sauce will bubble up, reduce, and form a glaze. If it isn't bubbling up and forming a glaze, turn the heat back on high and cook until the glaze is, well, "glazey."

step 7 Stack the collard leaves on top of each other, 3 to 4 at a time, and roll up.

step 8 Slice the roll in 1-inch segments.

step 9 Run your knife through the chopped collards to make smaller pieces, then add them to a wok with the water, lime juice, and salt.

step 10 Cover with any lid that will contain the collards and cook them over high heat for 3 to 4 minutes until the collards are steamed and tender.

step 11 For plating, arrange the collards on top of a bed of quinoa. Place the tofu over the top, drizzling any leftover sauce over the dish. Garnish with lime slices and mint leaves. Serve.

Tahini Lemon Rice and Beans

Here's a quick dish I made up for lunch to use some leftover kale and black beans. It's a departure from standard rice and beans, but I really enjoy it. The tahini in the sauce goes very well with the black beans, and the lemon lightens everything up a bit.

The sauce tastes stronger in the bowl than it does once you mix it with the rice, kale, and beans, so don't worry if it seems potent at first. I love adding raw, shredded carrot on top of dishes, not only for a nice crunch and sweetness, but for color too.

Tahini Lemon Rice and Beans

Makes 2 servings

step 1 Start cooking the rice according to the directions on the package.

step 2 Make the tahini lemon sauce by whisking together the soy sauce, tahini, lemon juice, rice vinegar, vegan Worcestershire sauce, water, and olive oil and set aside.

step 3 Heat a small amount of oil in a sauté pan and add the kale. When the kale starts to wilt, add the beans and seitan and heat through.

step 4 Add all of the sauce, stir, and turn off the heat and cover until the rice is finished cooking. (You could also wait to make this mixture until the rice is finished cooking.)

step 5 When the rice is finished, simply add it to the pan and toss to coat. Serve with shredded carrot on top.

Ingredients

1 cup brown rice

Tahini Lemon Sauce *(see recipe below)*

Vegetable oil for sautéeing

$1/2$ to 1 bunch kale, deveined and chopped

1 can black beans, rinsed and drained

6 ounces seitan, sliced in strips

Shredded carrot, to taste *(1 carrot works well)*

Tahini Lemon Sauce

$1/4$ cup soy sauce

$1/4$ cup tahini

2 tablespoons lemon juice

2 tablespoons rice vinegar

2 tablespoons vegan Worcestershire sauce *(see recipe on page 278)*

2 tablespoons water

2 tablespoons olive oil

Tamarind Tofu Cabbage Bowl

I f you already have the tamarind chutney made, this dish is wicked fast and easy. It's also a great way to use that cabbage hiding in your fridge.

Tamarind Tofu Cabbage Bowl

Makes 3 to 4 servings

step 1 Fry the tofu in the oil until browned on both sides. Set aside.

step 2 Combine the rice and carrots in a large bowl and toss well.

step 3 Sauté the cabbage over high heat with a little oil until slightly softened and browned in some places. Add the cabbage to the rice and carrots.

step 4 Make a sauce by mixing the tamarind chutney and tamari. Add the sauce and the tofu to the cabbage mixture and gently toss. Top with almonds. Serve warm.

Ingredients

1 12-ounce block firm tofu, pressed and cut into squares

2 to 3 tablespoons vegetable oil

2 cups cooked brown rice *(about 1 cup uncooked)*

1 carrot, shredded

4 cups shredded cabbage

2 tablespoons tamarind chutney *(see recipe on page 274)*

2 tablespoons tamari

1/4 cup toasted, sliced almonds

When reading these ingredients, you'll think a vegetable garden exploded all over my rice. You don't need to use every one of these veggies; if you want to skip one or two, feel free. Don't like mushrooms? Fine, leave 'em out. Can't find snow peas? Green beans or snap peas would be good instead.

This recipe involves a lot of chopping. It might take you 20 to 30 minutes to get all the veggies washed and prepped, depending on how quick you are with a knife. Feel free to use a food processor to make your life easier. I like the veggies to be chopped small, so you get a lot of interesting flavors and textures in each bite. Obviously, the smaller you chop, the more work it is. At the very least, chop the broccoli small so you don't end up with half-raw broccoli, unless you like that kind of thing. (Please note that all veggie measurements were taken after chopping.)

Vegetable Fried Rice

Makes 4 to 5 servings

step 1 Begin pressing the tofu, if you haven't already, and start the rice.

step 2 While the rice is cooking, chop the mushrooms, carrots, snow peas, zucchini, yellow and red bell peppers, broccoli, and kale and place them in separate piles or bowls. The carrots, peas, zucchini, and peppers can all go into one bowl to save space since you'll be adding them at the same time. If you're not shredding the carrots in a food processor, on a mandoline, or with a hand grater, you may want to keep the carrots separate so you can throw them into the wok earlier to soften. I cut my carrots thin enough that they're not too tough to chew even when raw. "Chunks" of carrots will definitely need more time in the wok.

step 3 Once all the veggies are prepared, heat up the wok. Add 1 to 2 tablespoons of oil on medium-high. Once the wok is hot, add the tofu carefully. Tofu + oil = HOT OIL SPLATTER. If you have a large mesh strainer, use that over your wok to play splatter defense. Use a long wooden spoon to agitate the tofu in the pan, frying for a few minutes while stirring it around until it's golden on all sides. If you have a decently seasoned wok, sticking won't be an issue, but if you don't, I'd recommend a little less oil and a nonstick pan.

Main Dishes

Ingredients

1 14-ounce block of extra-firm tofu, well pressed and cubed small *(2 cups) (may substitute seitan for the tofu; cut into small pieces/strips)*

1½ cups brown rice, uncooked

1 cup diced mushrooms, any kind

3 carrots, peeled and thinly sliced/shredded *(1 cup, packed)*

1 cup chopped snow peas, 1-inch pieces

1 cup ¼-inch diced zucchini

1 cup diced yellow bell pepper *(1 pepper)*

1 cup diced red bell pepper *(1 pepper)*

2 cups broccoli, chopped small

1 cup kale, shredded

2 to 3 tablespoons canola or peanut oil to use in wok

1 tablespoon soy sauce plus ½ teaspoon ginger powder, mixed *(or 1 teaspoon fresh ground ginger)*

Black pepper

3 tablespoons soy sauce, for the veggies

¼ cup low-sodium tamari or soy sauce *(or to taste)*

1 tablespoon mirin

1 tablespoon toasted sesame oil

Sesame seeds for garnish *(optional)*

step 4 Once the tofu is fried and golden, dump in the soy sauce/ginger mixture and stir until it bubbles up, reduces, and starts giving the tofu even more color. Use a slotted spoon to remove the tofu from the wok and place aside in a small bowl.

step 5 Add the broccoli to the pan (there should be oil left, but if there isn't, add a wee bit more). Cook, stirring, for 2 minutes or so. Add the mushrooms and cook for another 2 minutes. Add the kale and cook for another 2 minutes. Add the carrots, peas, zucchini, and peppers and cook for a few minutes more.

step 6 Grind some black pepper over the top. Add 3 tablespoons soy sauce and mix well. Cook until the mixture is steaming again and veggies are softened, 2 to 3 minutes.

step 7 The rice should be done by now. Add the rice to the wok and mix well. Add the tamari or soy sauce (or to taste), mirin, and sesame oil, mixing well until the alcohol smell of the mirin has dissipated, a minute or two. Taste, adding more soy sauce if you think it needs it. Serve immediately, placing tofu on top, sprinkled with sesame seeds.

chapter three

Appetizers

Chana Samosas

You can easily add both nutrition and flavor to classic potato Samosas by adding chickpeas, also known as chana. I've had both baked and fried Samosas, and there really is a huge difference in flavor and quality when you bite the bullet and deep-fry them. If you use a small, deep pot you can use less oil. If you do choose to bake them, I recommend doing a simpler (and flatter) half-moon shape, brushed with olive oil.

Chana Samosas

Makes 16 Samosas

step 1 Combine the flour, olive oil, water, salt, and cumin seeds and knead until smooth. Divide the dough into 8 equal balls, rolling each. Let the dough rest under lightly oiled plastic wrap while preparing filling (or for at least 20 minutes).

step 2 Boil the potatoes until tender and set aside.

step 3 Heat the oil and the margarine in a large skillet until hot. Add the cloves, cardamom pods, bay leaf, cinnamon stick, mustard seeds, and cumin seeds.

step 4 When the mustard seeds begin to pop, add the drained chickpeas. Cook until the chickpeas begin to brown.

step 5 Put the chickpea mixture and the previously cooked potatoes into a bowl and mash. Add the

2 cups all-purpose flour

1/3 cup olive oil

2/3 to 1 cup water

1/2 teaspoon salt

1/2 teaspoon cumin seeds

1 cup potato, diced and peeled

2 tablespoons olive oil

1 tablespoon Earth Balance margarine

2 cloves

2 cardamom pods

1 bay leaf

1 1 x 1-inch cinnamon stick

1/2 teaspoon mustard seeds

1/2 teaspoon cumin seeds

1 14-ounce can chickpeas, drained

1/4 teaspoon turmeric

1/2 teaspoon garam masala

1/2 teaspoon salt, to taste

Lemon juice, to taste

turmeric, garam masala, salt, and lemon juice, mix well.

step 6 Remove the balls of dough from the bowl and roll each of them into a disc that is 5 to 6 inches across, then slice in half.

step 7 Place half of a dough disc on your palm, with the straight edge aligned with your index finger as shown in the photo.

step 7 Form the dough into a cone and stuff with the filling.

step 8 With the seam in the center, close the Samosa by stretching and pinching the dough over the top. You can use a little bit of water to help seal the Samosa, if desired.

step 9 Set the Samosas aside, covered.

step 10 Heat a pot with several inches of oil to approximately 375°F. Fry the Samosas until golden brown. Drain on paper towels before serving. Serve warm with tamarind chutney (see recipe on page 274).

Vegan Yum Yum

Collard Dolmas and Cranberry Tahini

Cranberry tahini might seem like a strange flavor combination, but it's actually really delicious, especially paired with buttery lemon rice. After a quick boil, the collard leaves become tender and flexible and make for a colorful, sturdy wrap.

Collard Dolmas

6 large collard leaves, trimmed and blanched *(see below)*

1 cup long-grain rice, uncooked

2 to 3 tablespoons Earth Balance margarine

1/4 cup onion, finely diced

2 cloves garlic

1 tablespoon lemon juice

1/4 teaspoon salt

4 sprigs fresh thyme *(or 2 teaspoons of another herb, like parsley or mint)*

Zest of 1 lemon

Black pepper, to taste

Cranberry Tahini

1/2 cup tahini

1/2 cup water

1/2 cup dried cranberries *(plumped in hot water for 5 to 10 minutes)*

2 tablespoons lemon juice

1/4 teaspoon salt

Flavoring

2 tablespoons olive oil

1 tablespoon lemon juice

1/8 teaspoon salt

Collard Dolmas and Cranberry Tahini

Makes 6 pieces

step 1 Prepare the collards by removing two-thirds of each leaf's stem with scissors. Boil the leaves for 1 to 2 minutes, until bright green and tender. Drain and set aside.

step 2 Cook the rice according to package directions. Heat a skillet and melt the margarine in it, adding the onion and garlic and cooking until softened. Add the cooked rice and the lemon juice, salt, thyme, lemon zest, and black pepper and mix well.

step 3 To make the cranberry tahini, blend the tahini, water, cranberries, lemon juice, and salt in a food processor until smooth and set aside. Add additional water if necessary to get a smooth, diplike consistency.

step 4 Mix olive oil, lemon juice, and salt together in a small bowl.

step 5 Place one collard leaf down on a flat surface with the slit closest to you, facing vertically. Whatever side is facing down will be the outside of your dolma. With a pastry brush, brush the top of the leaf with the oil/lemon mixture.

step 6 Add ¼ to ½ cup of the rice to the bottom third and middle of the collard leaf. Fold in the sides, then fold up the bottom, and roll tightly. Serve immediately, at room temperature or slightly warm.

Corn Fritters

These cakes really take advantage of fresh summer corn, but frozen will work if it's all you have; simply defrost the kernels in warm water before adding to the recipe. The cakes come together in just minutes, so they're an easy addition to any meal. I use Old Bay seasoning, but if you don't have any, your favorite veggie seasoning will work perfectly, especially if it contains paprika and celery salt. Serve with a dollop of vegan sour cream, ketchup, or your favorite salad dressing. They pair well with a fresh salad and a glass of wine for a light meal.

Corn Fritters

Makes 10 to 12 fritters

step 1 Mix the flour, cornmeal, salt, baking powder, Old Bay Seasoning, cumin, and paprika together.

step 2 Add the soy milk and water to the dry ingredients and whisk until well combined. The batter should be thick, but not too thick to use a whisk.

step 3 Fold in the corn.

step 4 Heat a large, well-seasoned cast-iron or non-stick pan over medium-high heat with a few tablespoons of oil. When the oil is hot, take well-rounded tablespoons of the batter and cook cakes four at a time, gently spreading the cakes out with the back of a spoon before they set. Cook until golden brown, then flip and cook until the other side is golden. Drain on a paper towel before serving. Serve with herbed vegan sour cream, ketchup, or your own favorite sauce or gravy.

Ingredients

$1/2$ cup all-purpose flour

$1/2$ cup cornmeal

$3/4$ teaspoon salt

$1/2$ teaspoon baking powder

$1/2$ teaspoon Old Bay Seasoning

$1/4$ teaspoon cumin

$1/4$ teaspoon smoked paprika

$1/2$ cup soy milk

$1/4$ cup water

$1^1/2$ to 2 cups fresh corn *(in photo 1$^1/2$ cups were used)*

1 to 2 tablespoons of oil for frying

Eggplant and Basil Stuffed Tomatoes

This is an easy and elegant starter or side dish. If you use ripe, fresh summer produce, you'll be amazed how much flavor you can get without many ingredients. This is a perfect candidate for a balsamic reduction, drizzled over the top just before serving. If the tomatoes fall apart due to slight overcooking, don't worry. They're still tasty, just not as pretty. Serve them in a small bowl and no one will know the difference.

Eggplant and Basil Stuffed Tomatoes

Makes 6 servings as an appetizer or side

step 1 With the tip of a small paring knife, cut a cone out of the top of the tomatoes, removing the stem. Carefully remove a bit more of the inside until you see the seeds. Using a knife, spoon, or your fingers remove the seeds until you have an empty cavity. Drain them upside down on a paper towel until they're ready to stuff.

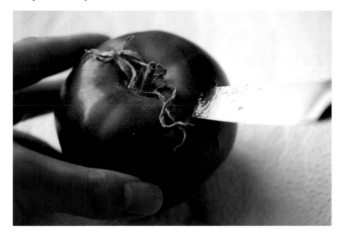

step 2 Preheat the oven to 400°F.

step 3 Toss the eggplant, salt, pepper, and olive oil in a large bowl.

step 4 Heat a large skillet or wok to high heat. Add the eggplant and cook, stirring occasionally, until the eggplant is very soft, no longer cubelike, and browned. It should be sort of sticky and mushy and much reduced in volume, which can take 10 minutes or longer.

step 5 Toast the bread, cube it, and then add it to the

6 ripe tomatoes, cored and drained *(see instructions)*

8 cups eggplant *(2 medium eggplants)*, unpeeled and cubed about the size of playing dice

1 teaspoon salt

Black pepper, to taste

$1/3$ cup olive oil *(use up to 2 more tablespoons if needed)*

4 slices bread, toasted and cubed *(white or your favorite)*

$1/2$ cup basil, chiffonade *(stack leaves, roll, and slice into thin strips)*

2 to 3 tablespoons balsamic vinegar for balsamic reduction, if desired *(see instructions on next page)*

eggplant along with the basil. Toss until well combined and turn off the heat.

step 6 Place the tomatoes in a baking dish that has been lightly coated with oil. Fill them completely full of stuffing, so that it's overflowing out of the tomatoes. Bake uncovered for 15 to 20 minutes, until the stuffing is browned on top and the tomatoes are tender. Drizzle with balsamic reduction if desired. Serve.

How to Make a Balsamic Reduction:

step 1 Heat ¼ cup of balsamic vinegar in a small saucepan. Don't stand right over the pan, because once it heats up, it will release vinegar fumes that are not fun to inhale.

step 2 Simmer this over medium heat until it has the consistency of syrup. (It takes me about 5 minutes to go from stone-cold pan to syrupy reduction.) You'll want to reduce it by half, so in the end you'll have only 2 tablespoons.

step 3 Use a rubber spatula to stir the vinegar. This will help you stir it once it starts to thicken, and you'll be able to see it getting syrupy because it'll start to coat the spatula. Don't overcook it, keeping in mind that it will thicken a little more once it has cooled down.

step 4 If you think it might be done, or close to done, take it off the heat immediately, place a little on a spoon, blow on it to cool it well, and taste it. It should be syrupy, sweet, tangy, and a little caramelized. You can always put it back on the heat to cook it more, but you can't really fix it if you overcook it. You can tell you're overcooking it if it starts to bubble up like sugar (really big, excited bubbles with an increase in volume). That's not what you want!

step 5 If it doesn't taste burned, but becomes too thick after it cools, try adding a little bit of water. That should loosen it up and get you back in business.

Miniature Napoleons with Eggplant Crème

When I lay awake at night, trying to sleep, I create recipes in my head. I usually start with a single ingredient and turn it over in my mind until something clicks. One night, I was contemplating the culinary fate of the two eggplants in my fridge and ruminating about how difficult eggplants can be in general. Undercooked eggplants usually have a "green" and a tough texture. When eggplant is good, it's so darn good, and when it's not, I personally find it gross. One of my memories from college is when my geology professor turned to me and remarked that you can judge the quality of a restaurant by the quality of its eggplant dishes. (Yes, I managed to talk food even with a geology professor.) Whether or not that's true, it speaks to what might be a common sentiment: eggplant can be a real pain!

So there I was, thinking about eggplants, and it hit me: eggplant mousse! (You'll notice I'm not calling it "mousse" in the recipe. After talking about the idea with several friends and seeing them wince at the term "eggplant mousse," I decided that it wasn't testing well and I'd have to change the name.) But just imagine eggplant, cubed and stir-fried until soft and golden, then blended with cashews and herbs until a rich, creamy, yet light spread forms. It's exquisite! And a lot tastier than "eggplant mousse" makes it sound.

Feeling the need to make something on the approachable side of fancy, as well as my ever-present obsession with teeny, tiny food, I decided to make napoleons that would pair well with the cremini mushroom (baby portobello) caps I had. You can easily make these on a larger scale with full-sized portobello mushrooms, but the tininess of the napoleons is a real draw for me. But I digress. To the recipe!

If you roast up more veggies than you need, you'll have an easier time matching diameters, and you'll have leftovers for a really tasty grilled veggie sandwich the next day. Did I mention the eggplant makes a great sandwich spread and filling for ravioli?

Miniature Napoleons
with Eggplant Crème

Makes 12 miniature napoleons with leftover crème

step 1 Preheat the oven to 300°F.

step 2 Place the sliced tomatoes and zucchini on a baking sheet; I use a baking mat, similar to a Silpat, but foil or parchment will work too.

step 3 Spray the vegetables with oil to coat (or brush with oil if you don't have the spray stuff). Sprinkle with salt, pepper, and dried Italian herbs. Bake for 1 hour and 15 minutes, until the veggies look dehydrated and smaller.

step 4 Place the mushrooms on the same baking sheet, upside down. Fill the centers with a little tamari,

Ingredients

Special Equipment Needed:

Piping bag *(the type used for cake decorating)* or a 1-quart plastic bag

Roasted Vegetables:

3 to 4 plum tomatoes, sliced thick *(at least 12 slices, between $1/4$ inch and $1/2$ inch)*

1 zucchini, sliced thick *(at least 12 slices)*

Cooking oil spray

Salt, to taste

Black pepper, to taste

Dried Italian herbs *(your choice; I use a mix of marjoram, basil, oregano, and rosemary)*

12 cremini mushroom caps, de-stemmed and brushed clean

Tamari or soy sauce, to taste

Eggplant Crème:

2 eggplants

2 tablespoons extra virgin olive oil, more if needed

$1/2$ teaspoon salt

(Ingredients continued on next page)

⅔ cup raw, unsalted cashews

1 teaspoon dried Italian herbs *(your choice; I like basil, marjoram, oregano, and rosemary)*

2 or 3 cloves garlic, minced *(optional)*

Garnish:

Roasted tomato

Fresh basil *(at least one leaf per napoleon)*

2 to 3 tablespoons olive oil

1 to 2 teaspoons balsamic vinegar

no more than ½ to 1 teaspoon. They'll look like this:

step 5 Spray them thoroughly with the cooking oil spray and bake for 30 minutes, or until tender. Remove and let cool with the tomatoes and zucchini.

step 6 While the vegetables are baking, prepare the eggplant crème. Cut the ends off of the eggplants and remove the skin. Cube the eggplants and place them on a large dish on top of three paper towels (you'll probably need to do this in batches). Microwave the eggplant on high for about 8 minutes, until it is soft and the paper towels have absorbed most of the moisture. (This will prevent the eggplant from absorbing so much oil while cooking.)

step 7 Heat a seasoned wok or nonstick pan with 2 tablespoons of olive oil. Add the eggplant and sauté for 5 to 10 minutes over medium-high heat until very soft and browned. Add the eggplant to the work bowl of a food processor fitted with a steel blade. Add the salt, cashews, herbs, and the garlic (if using) and process for several minutes until very smooth; it should be the consistency of creamy hummus. Season to taste, if needed, and then place the eggplant crème in a piping bag or a 1-quart plastic bag with one of the corners cut off.

step 8 To assemble, put a little dot of eggplant crème on the plate where you want the napoleon to be. This will act as an anchor (or the tastiest glue in the world).

step 9 Place a tomato on top of the anchor and pipe more eggplant crème on the top. Not too much!

step 10 Add a slice of zucchini, then another layer of eggplant crème. Top with an upside-down mushroom cap and place a dab of egg-plant crème where the stem was.

step 11 For garnish, add a small piece of roasted tomato and a basil-leaf crown. Put a thin layer of olive oil in the bottom of the dish, surrounding the napoleons. Drizzle balsamic vinegar into the oil, and you'll create pretty, contrasting dots. Serve warm or at room temperature.

Onigiri

Onigiri, or rice balls, are a popular Japanese snack or light meal. They're great for picnics or packed lunches, and they're easily customizable. They require few ingredients and aren't difficult to make, but it may take a few tries to get used to shaping them. The rice is usually shaped with bare hands, which can be uncomfortable (since the rice needs to be hot!) and quite messy if you're not careful. The method given below uses moistened plastic wrap and greatly reduces the mess and difficulty of shaping. If you live near a Japanese market, you can find inexpensive plastic shaping molds there.

Onigiri are traditionally filled with umeboshi, also called pickled plums. They not only provide a burst of flavor, but they are also used to prevent the rice from spoiling in packed lunches on hot summer days. I don't really like umeboshi myself, but you may wish to include one in the center of your onigiri. You can fill them with anything you wish, although salty and sour things are traditional. One of my testers suggested spinach sautéed with garlic and sugar, which is another popular filling for rice balls in Japan; it's neither sour nor salty, but it's definitely tasty!

Vegan Yum Yum

Onigiri

Makes 8 pieces

step 1 Cook the rice and let it steam for 5 to 10 minutes before opening the rice cooker or removing the lid of your pot. Add the rice to a large bowl and coat it with the sushi or rice vinegar to taste (you won't need more than 1/4 cup for every 2 dry cups of prepared rice). Shape the hot rice as desired (see directions below).

Shaping the Onigiri:

step 1 Get organized. You want to have everything you need ready before the rice is finished cooking. Prepare a clear work surface for shaping the onigiri. Have a plate covered in plastic wrap, lightly coated in oil, on which to place your finished onigiri.

step 2 Line the shaping bowl with plastic wrap. Wet the plastic wrap with some cool, salty water, sprinkling it in with your fingers. Dump out the extra water.

step 3 Using a spoon, loosely fill the bowl with rice. If

Ingredients

Rice:

2 cups dry sushi rice *(short-grain rice, or glutenous)* *

3 to 4 tablespoons sushi vinegar or regular rice vinegar

*Note: Be sure to use the amount of water recommended on the rice package. As a general rule of thumb, short-grain rice cooks best with a 1:1.25 rice-to-water ratio.

Fillings and Flavorings (all optional):

Miso

Other pickled items

Sautéed spinach, flavored with garlic and sugar

Soy sauce *(for grilled/broiled/fried yaki onigiri)*

Umeboshi

Wrappings and Decorations:

Nori sheets, dried

Black sesame seeds

you're using fillings, fill the bowl halfway, lightly pack the rice, add the filling in the center, then top with more rice and proceed.

step 4 Scoop the rice up in the plastic wrap and begin to compress it. Follow the directions below for the shape you desire to make.

Making the Triangle Onigiri:

step 1 Begin forming the rice into a triangle shape, starting with a point at the top. The rice will bulge out the front at first.

step 2 Flatten the front and continue shaping your triangle. The points should be rounded, and the front and back should be flat. Continue shaping until it's about 95 percent done.

step 3 Wet your hands thoroughly with the salty water to prevent the rice from sticking to you. Remove the triangle from the plastic wrap. Put the finishing touches on the shape, being careful not to press too hard so as not to break it.

step 4 Place shaped rice aside on lightly oiled plastic wrap while you finish shaping the rest of the rice. You can create all sorts of shapes using this method.

Decorating

Decorating serves two purposes. Most obviously, it makes the onigiri look nice. However, the decorations also make the surface of the rice (or a portion of it) less sticky for easier handling while eating. They also provide a little bit of flavor.

Vegan Yum Yum

Nori-wrapped Onigiri:

step 1 Place a sheet of nori, shiny side down, on a flat surface. Lightly rub or spray it with salty water until just damp—it will absorb the water almost immediately. You're not trying to soak the seaweed; you just want to soften it so that it doesn't crack when folding.

step 2 Place the onigiri in the center of your nori.

step 3 Draw the edges into the center, pulling it taut as you go.

step 4 Place the onigiri seam side down when finished. It should dry slightly and not unwrap when handled. You can also wrap the shapes in strips of moistened nori.

Sesame Onigiri:

Black sesame seeds look great on white rice. You can use just a few or coat the entire surface.

Yaki Onigiri:

This one is my favorite! I prefer the broiler method, but the stove top will work, too.

Broiler method: Place the onigiri on oiled foil and broil until top is lightly browned. Flip and repeat. Brush soy sauce on the top, then broil for another minute or two. Flip, brush remaining side with soy sauce, broil, and serve.

Stove-top method: Place the onigiri in an oiled pan and fry until bottom is lightly browned. Brown both sides, then add soy sauce to each side and brown again. Each will have fried twice, once for initial browning and once after basting with soy sauce. Serve immediately.

Sesame Ginger Seitan Dumplings

Dumplings seem difficult, but there's no reason you can't enjoy them at home. I've kept the filling simple for two reasons: One, food doesn't need to be complicated to be awesome, and two, you're going to be filling the things by hand, so why take more time than you need to? With only a small amount of practice, I can fill ten of these in five minutes, without rushing through any beat-the-clock test. If you stay organized, these are really fun to make! Once you make dumplings the first time, I promise you'll be dreaming up new fillings of your own and making them again and again.

These make a great presentation for dinner parties if you serve them in a bamboo steamer with ginger and sesame oil (see page 110). My bamboo steamer only cost $15 at a local Asian market, but a regular steamer will work just fine. You can also boil or braise your dumplings.

Vegan Yum Yum

Sesame Ginger Seitan Dumplings

Makes approximately 40 dumplings

Prepare the filling:

step 1 Remove the outer leaves of the cabbage and discard. Then remove enough leaves to line your steamer. Line the steamer and lightly oil the leaves to provide a nonstick surface for your dumplings.

step 2 Shred the remaining cabbage in the bowl of a food processor to make 2$\frac{1}{2}$ cups total.

step 3 Chop the seitan roughly and add to the processor. Pulse until only small chunks of seitan and cabbage remain. Scrape out into a mixing bowl. If the mixture is wet from the cabbage, squeeze out the excess liquid.

step 4 Add the mirin, tamari, sesame oil, and ginger to the cabbage/seitan mixture and combine well. Set aside to let the flavors incorporate and then prepare the sauce.

The sauce:

Combine the soy sauce, lemon juice, rice vinegar, and water. The sauce may be served like this if a traditional dipping sauce is needed. If a thicker sauce is preferred (as shown in the main photo), add the cornstarch and water mixture and heat over medium heat in a small saucepan, whisking until thickened and no longer milky. Set aside to cool.

Ingredients

Filling:

2$\frac{1}{2}$ cups shredded Napa cabbage

8 ounces seitan *(about 1$\frac{1}{2}$ cups)*

1 teaspoon mirin

1 teaspoon reduced-sodium tamari

1 teaspoon toasted sesame oil

1 teaspoon fresh grated ginger

Sauce:

$\frac{1}{4}$ cup soy sauce

2 teaspoons lemon juice

2 teaspoons seasoned rice vinegar

2 teaspoons water

3 teaspoon water plus 1 teaspoon cornstarch *(thick sauce option only)*

Dumplings:

1 package dumpling skins

1 small bowl of water

Cooking oil or oil spray

4 moistened paper towels, or two damp kitchen towels

Fill the dumplings:

step 1 Place 1¹/₂ to 2 teaspoons of filling in the middle of your dumpling skin. Dip your finger in the bowl of water and wet the edges of the skin.

step 2 Gently fold the skin up to form a semicircle, sealing the edges by pressing with your fingers.

step 3 Make one fold in the middle and press to seal. Make two more folds, one to either side of the first fold. Press to seal both. You can push the bottom of the dumpling on the table to create a flat base so the dumpling can sit upright.

step 4 Repeat until all of the filling has been used. Keep the completed dumplings under moist paper towels or kitchen towels and the stack of skins under another to prevent them from drying out while you are working.

Steam the dumplings:

Place the dumplings on the oiled cabbage leaves in your steamer, adding as many as you can without allowing them to touch. Bring the water to boil,

place steamer on top, and cook for 6 minutes. Remove immediately and serve.

Serving tip: If you're using a bamboo steamer, bring it to the table for serving. If you are serving the dumplings in the steamer, consider adding three or four fresh ginger slices and oiling the leaves with just enough sesame oil to coat them before steaming. This will create a fragrant burst of steam when it is opened in front of your guests. Serve with dipping sauce or glaze.

ellooo! Can you say "So easy"? You will make this for friends and they will love you. This dish is sweet, salty, spicy, and crispy all at the same time. It can easily be served as a side dish instead. I leave the tops on my sugar snap peas for better presentation, but you can trim them off if you don't want to bother with them while eating.

This recipe won't be as good if your sugar snap peas aren't fresh, so try to find the freshest ones you can. Peas are one of the most sensitive vegetables around; the longer they sit after picking, the soggier and less sweet they become. Local farmers' markets are often the best place to purchase peas since you're almost guaranteed the peas were picked earlier that day.

4 cups fresh sugar snap peas *(12 ounces)*

1¹/₂ tablespoons soy sauce

1¹/₂ tablespoons agave nectar or sugar

1¹/₂ tablespoons black sesame seeds

³/₄ teaspoon red pepper flakes

1 teaspoon cornstarch

1 tablespoon water

Sugar and Spice Snap Peas

Makes 4 appetizer portions

step 1 Trim the peas if desired by pinching the tops and pulling the "zipper"; they shouldn't open on you. If a few give you trouble, just ignore them, since you can eat the whole pod anyway.

step 2 Mix together the soy sauce, agave, sesame seeds, red pepper flakes, and the premixed cornstarch/water mixture.

step 3 Heat a wok to high and add the peas. Add the water and quickly cover the wok with a lid; the lid should be large enough so as not to touch the peas, but it doesn't need to fit around the top of the wok; it can sit inside the rim a bit. The idea is to keep the steam in well enough to cook the peas.

step 4 After 1 to 2 minutes, remove the cover and stir the peas until all of the water has evaporated and the peas look dry. Add the sauce until it bubbles up and reduces within 1 to 2 minutes or less, coating the peas. Serve immediately.

Vegan Yum Yum

chapter four

Salads

Apple Cranberry Salad with Country-Fried Seitan

My husband calls salads like these "tossed sandwiches," and I'm inclined to agree with him. Our favorite salads don't include just lettuce; they usually include our favorite veggies, a tasty homemade dressing, tofu or seitan, and sometimes fruit and nuts. We don't make wimpy "house salads" with a few leaves of lettuce and some sliced tomatoes. Our salads are entire meals that look like they've exploded in the bowl. Feel free to be creative with the ingredients to find a salad that suits your tastes best.

While I think this is a perfect salad, the fried seitan is really tasty and works well as the staple of a meal (say, with some mashed potatoes and gravy? Yes, please!) or even as a sandwich. Whatever your preference, it's crispy and delicious and meant to resemble country-fried chicken.

I've given directions for making the seitan from scratch (it's not hard!), but any premade seitan should work. The main benefit of making it from scratch is that you control the flavor and texture, but feel free to sub store-bought seitan if you want.

The fried seitan relies on Old Bay, a wonderful commercial spice blend that you should seek out if you've never tried it. You can find it at any major grocery store, and it gives the perfect seasoning to the fried seitan. You can make the seitan ahead of time (up to a few days in advance) and then deep-fry it when you're ready. I've included instructions on how to make the seitan first, followed by frying instructions, and then the rest of the salad ingredients.

Creamy Almond Dijon Dressing

$1/2$ cup sliced almonds *(blanched or raw)*

$1/2$ cup water

2 tablespoons nutritional yeast

$1^1/2$ teaspoons tamari or low-sodium soy sauce

1 tablespoon fresh lemon juice

2 teaspoons Dijon or stone-ground mustard

$1/2$ teaspoon Old Bay Seasoning

Salad mix

1 head lettuce *(Romaine, green, butter, whatever)*

1 Granny Smith apple, thinly sliced

$1/2$ cup dried cranberries

Seitan cutlet

1 fried seitan cutlet *(see recipes on page 117-118)*

Apple Cranberry Salad with Country-Fried Seitan

step 1 Blend all of the dressing ingredients together in a high-speed blender until smooth and no pieces of almonds remain. You may refrigerate the dressing while you're preparing the lettuce and apple.

step 2 Clean the lettuce and tear into bite-size pieces. Toss the lettuce with the salad dressing and place on a plate. Add the sliced apples and dried cranberries. Place 1 fried seitan cutlet on top and drizzle with more dressing. Serve while the seitan is still warm. Refrigerate the leftover seitan for later use.

Chicken-Style Seitan

Makes 4 cutlets

step 1 Mix the wheat gluten, yeast, and Old Bay Seasoning together in a small bowl.

step 2 In a different small bowl, combine the water, tamari, soy milk, and olive oil, stirring well.

step 3 Add the wet ingredients to the dry and knead until a dough forms. Add more liquid if needed to moisten all of the dry ingredients.

step 4 Knead the dough a few times on your counter and form it into a ball. Cut the ball into quarters, forming four triangular wedges. Squish, pound, and pull the wedges into 1/2-inch-thick cutlets, taking your time to shape them and letting them rest first if they won't stretch out.

step 5 Once they're the proper thickness, put a large, high-walled skillet on medium heat, adding the water and bouillon cube to make a braising broth. Once it starts simmering, add the cutlets and turn down the heat to low and cover. It's important that you *do not* boil the cutlets. Check several times to make sure the broth is just barely simmering. Boiling isn't a disaster, but it will change the texture of the cutlets, making them spongier and rubbery.

step 6 Simmer covered for 20 to 30 minutes, flipping halfway through. You can now refrigerate the cutlets in their broth for later use, or fry them immediately. I personally think cutlets that have been refrigerated overnight before frying have a better texture, but you can use them right away if you need to.

Ingredients

Chicken-Style Seitan

1 1/2 cups vital wheat gluten

2 tablespoons nutritional yeast

1 teaspoon Old Bay Seasoning

3/4 cup cold water

1 tablespoon tamari or low-sodium soy sauce

3 tablespoons soy milk

1 tablespoon olive oil

Braising broth

2 cups water

1 vegetable bouillon cube

Fried Seitan

32 ounces high-heat oil for frying *(canola, peanut, etc.)*

Seasoned dry mix

1 1/2 cups all-purpose flour

1/4 cup nutritional yeast

3 teaspoons Old Bay Seasoning

4 teaspoons baking powder

Wet mix

1/3 cup seasoned dry mix *(from above)*

1/4 cup water

1/4 cup soy milk *(or water)*

3 tablespoons mustard *(Dijon or stone-ground)*

Ingredients

Country-Fried Seitan

4 chicken-style seitan cutlets (recipe on page 117)

step 1 Heat the oil to 350°F in a 10-inch skillet (cast iron is best).

step 2 Mix together the flour, yeast, and Old Bay Seasoning.

step 3 In a separate bowl, mix together 1/3 cup of the dry mix, water, soy milk, and mustard.

step 4 Add the baking powder to the remaining dry ingredients and mix well.

step 5 When the oil is heated, dip a seitan cutlet into the wet mix, coating well. Then dredge the cutlet in the dry mix and gently slip it into the oil. Fry for 2 to 3 minutes on each side, until golden brown and crispy. Drain well on a paper towel and slice to serve, if desired.

Vegan Yum Yum

Caesar Salad

A good vegan caesar salad dressing is hard to find. When I make this, I add garlic to my husband's portion, but leave it out of mine. It'd be extra tasty with some Country-Fried Seitan (page 118) sliced on top, but I like the dressing enough to eat it plain. If you've never made your own croutons before, you're in for a surprise; they're so easy and tasty, you'll wonder why you've never made them before!

1 head of Romaine lettuce

Croutons

3 cups sourdough bread cubes

Olive oil

Salt, to taste

Herbs *(an Italian-type blend works nicely, such as basil, marjoram, and oregano)*

Caesar Dressing

¼ cup sliced almonds

¼ cup plus 1 tablespoon miso

1 tablespoon plus 2 teaspoons Dijon mustard

2 tablespoons vegan Worcestershire sauce *(see page 278)*

2 cloves garlic

1 tablespoon white wine vinegar

4 pinches salt

½ block silken tofu *(about 6 ounces)*

¼ cup olive oil

1 tablespoon nutritional yeast *(optional)*

2 tablespoons water or more oil, to thin

Caesar Salad

One head of lettuce makes a dinner-size portion for two or several starter salads

step 1 Wash the lettuce, remove the outer leaves, and leave in the drainer to dry.

step 2 Preheat the oven to 400°F. Toss the bread cubes in olive oil to coat and then sprinkle lightly with salt and the dried herbs of your choice. Bake for 15 minutes or until crispy but not browned. Let cool and set aside. (Keep in an airtight container if making ahead of time.)

step 2 Rip the lettuce into bite-size pieces and place in a large bowl.

step 3 Make the dressing by blending the almonds, miso, mustard, Worcestershire, garlic, vinegar, salt, tofu, olive oil, yeast, and water in a food processor or blender until smooth.

step 4 Toss the lettuce with the dressing and add the croutons right before serving.

Golden Chickpea and Artichoke Salad

This is a very easy, quick, high-protein dish that's great as a side or even a whole meal. Sautéing the chickpeas brings out a lovely nutty flavor, almonds add crunch, and fresh parsley and artichokes round out the dish.

1 tablespoon oil

1 15-ounce can chickpeas, drained

5 to 7 artichoke hearts, drained and sliced length-wise

1/4 to 1/3 cup sliced almonds *(toasted if desired)*

1 teaspoon lemon juice

1/4 teaspoon salt

2 tablespoons fresh chopped parsley

Golden Chickpea and Artichoke Salad

Makes one meal or 4 side salads

step 1 Heat the oil in a seasoned wok or a cast-iron skillet. Add the chickpeas and cook on medium-high for 10 minutes, stirring only occasionally to prevent burning, until the chickpeas are golden brown all over. When done, put them into a large mixing bowl and set aside.

step 2 Add more oil to the pan and cook the sliced artichoke hearts until browned. Add them to the bowl of chickpeas.

step 3 Toast the almonds in a dry skillet (if desired) and then grind them in a food processor. Add the almonds to the artichokes and chickpeas. Season the salad with lemon juice and salt and stir in the chopped parsley. Serve warm or at room temperature, adjusting the seasoning if needed.

Glazed Green Bean Salad

This easy green bean salad is the perfect summer side dish. It keeps well, so feel free to make it ahead of time and store it in the fridge. It's perfect for picnics too!

1 pound fresh green beans
(thinner "haricot verts" are preferred)

1 tablespoon cooking sherry
(white wine would work, too)

1 tablespoon tamari

1 tablespoon maple syrup

1 teaspoon cornstarch

1/3 cup pine nuts

Black pepper, to taste

Glazed Green Bean Salad

Makes 4 servings as a side dish

step 1 Trim green beans to 2 inches (I like to trim them on an angle to dress up the salad a bit). Steam *gently* until tender-crisp, just a few minutes, then fully submerge in ice-cold water to stop the cooking process. Dry well and set aside in a large bowl.

step 2 To make the glaze, mix the cooking sherry, tamari, maple syrup, and cornstarch together until the cornstarch is dissolved. Place the glaze in a small saucepan and whisk constantly over high heat until the sauce turns clear and thickens. (This happens fast, so be on your toes.) Remove the sauce using a rubber spatula, pouring it onto the beans, getting every single bit of sauce out of the pot.

step 3 Place the pine nuts in a dry sauté pan over medium heat. Toast the nuts until golden brown, being careful not to burn them! You'll see the nuts turn slightly shiny just before they start to brown. Remove the toasted nuts from the pan and place into a mortar and pestle or food processor to crush them. (If you don't have a mortar and pestle or food processor, you could put them into a bag and crush them with a rolling pin or skillet.)

step 4 Toss the glazed beans with the crushed nuts. Grate fresh black pepper over the top, to taste. Serve immediately or refrigerate for later.

Vegan Yum Yum

Grilled Pear, Walnut, and Cabbage Salad

Who says cabbage can't be fancy? This elegant salad is perfect for entertaining. The grilled pear and the sweet dressing are set off by salty-sweet walnuts that play the part of croutons in this salad. All of the flavors work really well together and nothing overwhelms. Some black mission figs would be a great addition, if they are in season.

The walnuts, dressing, and cabbage can be prepared ahead of time. Dress the cabbage an hour or so before serving and refrigerate. The dressing does double duty here as a grill sauce for the pears. If you make the pears last minute, you can serve them slightly warm and still fragrant from the grill.

1 cup walnuts

1/2 teaspoon Earth Balance margarine

1 teaspoon soy sauce

3/4 teaspoon sugar

1 recipe Lemon and Brown Sugar Dressing *(see below)*

1 head green cabbage *(the round, pale green variety)*

1 tablespoon poppy seeds

1 Bosc pear, firmly ripe

8 black mission figs, quartered *(if in season)*

Lemon Brown Sugar Dressing

Makes scant 1/2 cup

3 tablespoons fresh lemon juice

3 tablespoons light brown sugar

1/2 teaspoon kosher salt

1 teaspoon soy sauce

Fresh cracked black pepper, to taste

1/4 cup peanut oil

Grilled Pear, Walnut, and Cabbage Salad

Makes 4 large plate servings or 8 starter plates

step 1 Put the walnuts and margarine into a nonstick skillet. Cook on medium, tossing the walnuts until they are coated in the margarine. (You should have just enough to make them shiny, but you shouldn't see any pools of oil.) Add the soy and sugar sauce to the pan and be ready to mix like crazy. Now, mix like crazy! The soy sauce should bubble up and coat the walnuts. Turn off the heat and let the walnuts cool on parchment paper or a slightly oiled surface (so they won't stick).

step 2 To make the dressing, whisk together the lemon juice, brown sugar, salt, soy sauce, and black pepper in a small bowl until completely combined, making sure the salt and sugar have dissolved. Slowly drizzle in the 1/4 cup of peanut oil while whisking vigorously. Set aside.

step 3 Quarter the cabbage. Remove the outer leaves and cores. Shred into thin strips and dress with just enough dressing to coat, 4 to 6 tablespoons. Add poppy seeds, mix, and refrigerate.

step 4 Heat the grill. Halve the pear. Using a melon baller or a 1/2-teaspoon measure, carve out a neat ball, removing any seeds. Cut each piece in half again (4 pieces) and in half again (8 pieces). Use one of the seed balls to test the heat of the grill: dip it in the dressing and press it down on the grill; if it has grill marks after about a minute, the grill is ready.

step 5 Gently toss the pears in the leftover dressing and grill. Place them at a 45-degree angle and grill for 1 minute; then turn them 90 degrees and grill for one more minute to get a crosshatch. Grill on the other side in the same manner and remove the pears to a plate.

step 6 Plate them by laying down a bed of cabbage. Lay the pears (and the figs, if you're using them) over that and sprinkle with the walnuts. Serve.

Pea Tendril and Daikon Noodle Salad

I love this recipe because it looks super fancy, but it's super easy. I realize pea tendrils are seasonal and hard to find, so you can use any delicate, small-leaved salad green. I've given some suggestions in the recipe, but use whatever you find or that inspires you. Pea tendrils are particularly nice, though; look for them in early June. I recommend you serve this salad with chopsticks if you have them. They make the salad easy and fun to eat, and it plays well with the Asian-themed ingredients.

Vegan Yum Yum

Pea Tendril and Daikon Noodle Salad

Makes 4 servings

step 1 Make the dressing by whisking together the soy sauce, soy milk, sesame oil, agave nectar, vinegar, ginger, cayenne pepper, and black pepper. Then slowly drizzle in the canola or peanut oil while whisking vigorously, until emulsified. You can do this in a running blender or food processor if you prefer. Chill until ready to use.

step 2 Using a regular vegetable peeler, shave off long "noodles" from the daikon radishes. Turn the daikons while shaving to get fairly consistent widths; if you stay in the same place for too long your noodles will get wider and wider!

step 3 Toss the noodles gently with the pea tendrils or chosen greens, then pile high on the serving plates. Arrange if desired, and add more greens on top if needed. Sprinkle with sesame seeds and drizzle with dressing. Serve immediately!

Sesame Soy Dressing

Makes approximately ³/₄ cup

3 tablespoons soy sauce

2 tablespoons soy milk

1 tablespoon toasted sesame oil

1 tablespoon agave nectar

1 tablespoon apple cider vinegar

¹/₄ teaspoon powdered ginger *(or 1 teaspoon fresh ginger, or to taste)*

1 small dash cayenne pepper

Black pepper, to taste

6 tablespoons canola or peanut oil

2 daikon radishes, about 6 to 7 inches long and 2 inches in diameter, peeled

4¹/₂ cups of pea tendrils *(or substitute baby spinach, watercress, mâche, or arugula)*

Black sesame seeds, for garnish

Ingredients

chapter five

Side Dishes and Light Meals

Apple Cider Brussels Sprouts

I didn't know I liked Brussels sprouts until I was an adult. I think they get a bad rap, so if you haven't tried them for a while, give this recipe a go. If you overcook sprouts, you bring out their unpleasant tasting and smelling sulfur compounds. This method leaves the sprouts crisp and sweet, with a slightly nutty aftertaste. This is my absolute favorite way to eat sprouts!

Apple Cider Brussels Sprouts

Makes 2 to 4 side servings

step 1 Trim the ends off of the Brussels sprouts, remove loose and blemished leaves, and then halve.

step 2 Heat the oil in a very large sauté pan, allowing the pan to get really hot, but not smoking. Place the Brussels sprouts in, cut side down, and let them cook for 1 to 2 minutes until seared with some color but not cooked through. Turn down the heat to medium low, add the apple cider, and cover. Cook for 4 minutes, or until just tender; a knife inserted into the stem should go in with a little resistance, and the Brussels sprouts should be bright green. Remove them from the pan with a slotted spoon and place them into a large bowl, leaving the liquid behind in the pan. If a couple of stray leaves remain, that's fine.

step 3 Turn down the heat a bit more and add the margarine, mustard, and salt. When the margarine is melted, sprinkle in the flour and whisk until smooth.* Turn up the heat and keep whisking until the sauce is thickened, another couple of seconds. Pour the sauce over sprouts, toss, and serve immediately.

*Note: If the pan is too hot when you add the flour, you'll get a lumpy sauce no matter what, because the flour will cook and form lumps as soon as it hits the pan instead of dissolving evenly and then thickening to form a smooth, silky sauce. I recommend waiting for the pan to cool a bit, or you can whisk the flour into a small amount of water or apple juice, so that the flour is moist before you add it to the pan. The most important step is to keep whisking until the sauce is smooth and thick.

Ingredients

1½ pounds Brussels sprouts, trimmed and halved

3 tablespoons vegetable oil

1 cup apple cider or apple juice

4 tablespoons Earth Balance margarine

1 teaspoon Dijon mustard

¼ to ½ teaspoon salt

1 tablespoon all-purpose flour

Candied Lime Sweet Potatoes

This is just a simple candied sweet potato dish, but the addition of lime really makes it special. You can throw fresh parsley on the top, or if you're feeling a bit less traditional, fresh cilantro. I think people forget sometimes that the cut of the vegetable you choose is really important for the overall texture and flavor of a dish. This dish will almost definitely work without slicing the sweet potatoes so thin, but the delicate candied rounds give it an elegant appearance and uniform texture. Every bite becomes infused with the sweet lime syrup. I used a Japanese mandoline that allowed me to quickly slice the sweet potatoes evenly and efficiently. If I was working with only a knife, I wouldn't attempt to get slices this thin and accurate. Thicker coins or chunks will work just as well, but if you have a mandoline, this is the perfect dish to use it for. The slicing disc of your food processor will also work.

Vegan Yum Yum

Candied Lime Sweet Potatoes

Makes 4 servings

step 1 Preheat the oven to 400°F. Slice the sweet potatoes thin, about 1/8 inch, with a mandoline or a food processor.

step 2 In a bowl, mix together the sugar, molasses, salt, lime juice, lime zest, and ginger to form a paste.

step 3 Coat the sliced sweet potatoes well with the lime sugar mixture.

step 4 In an oiled casserole dish, arrange the coated slices in overlapping rows in one layer. Dot with margarine, sprinkle with pepper, and cover the dish tightly with two layers of aluminum foil.

step 5 Bake for 30 minutes, then remove foil and bake uncovered for an additional 10 minutes. It's okay if it looks a little watery when you remove the foil; it'll reduce and form a nice glaze during the rest of the baking.

step 6 To finish, turn on the broiler and broil until the tops of the sweet potatoes are brown. Remove, sprinkle with black pepper and parsley or cilantro, and serve immediately.

Ingredients

2 sweet potatoes, peeled

1/2 cup sugar

1 teaspoon molasses

1/2 teaspoon salt

1 tablespoon fresh lime juice *(no bottled stuff!)*

Zest from 1 small lime

1/2 teaspoon minced ginger or 1/4 teaspoon ginger powder *(optional)*

Earth Balance margarine, for dotting

Black pepper, to taste

Parsley or cilantro, for garnish

Coconut Lime Tofu

This simple baked tofu is easy to prepare with ingredients you probably have on hand. It's a great addition to salads, sandwiches, noodle dishes, or anything else you can dream up.

Coconut Lime Tofu

Makes 1 block

step 1 Preheat the oven to 400°F. Oil an 8-x-8-inch baking dish.

step 2 Cut tofu into 8 equal pieces as follows: Lay the block in front of you, widthwise. Cut into 4 equal slabs. Lay each slab on its side and cut in half, lengthwise, forming a skinny rectangle (see photo).

step 3 Add the coconut milk, soy sauce, lime, sugar, and lime zest to a blender or food processor and blend well.

step 4 Add the tofu to a casserole dish and pour the marinade over it. Bake for 25 minutes, flip, and bake for an additional 10 minutes, or until the vast majority of the marinade has been absorbed and evaporated. Remove from the oven and let it rest until it has cooled a bit before serving.

Ingredients

1 14-ounce package tofu, drained and well pressed

$2/3$ cup coconut milk

$1/4$ cup soy sauce

1 half lime, peeled

2 teaspoons sugar

Zest of 1 lime

Creamy Tomato Barley Risotto

his is a comforting side dish that will go perfectly with any Italian-themed meal. The toothy barley is just as satisfying as real risotto without all the bothersome stirring. It takes about 40 minutes to make, but most of that is downtime, so it's a great dish to have cooking away on the back burner while you prepare the rest of your meal.

Creamy Tomato Barley Risotto

Makes 4 side dishes

step 1 Put the barley, olive oil, oregano, and basil into a cold medium-size pot that has a tight-fitting lid. Turn the heat to medium-high and stir until barley is coated in the oil.

step 2 Once the barley begins sizzling (about a minute), add the garlic. Cook for another minute or so, then add the tomatoes, soy milk, water, yeast, miso, and salt. Bring to a gentle boil, then cover and turn down the heat to just hotter than the lowest setting. Cook for 20 minutes. After 20 minutes, stir well, re-cover, and cook for another 15 minutes, stirring once more toward the end. The mixture should be creamy but not soupy, and the barley should be cooked all the way through but not mushy. Serve immediately.

1 cup pearled barley

1 tablespoon olive oil

$1/2$ teaspoon dried oregano

$1/2$ teaspoon dried basil

1 clove garlic, minced

$1^1/2$ cups fresh or canned diced tomatoes *(14.5-ounce can)* blended or mashed a bit

1 cup soy milk

$1/2$ cup water

$1/4$ cup nutritional yeast

3 tablespoons miso *(mellow or white)* mixed with 3 tablespoons water

$1/4$ to $1/2$ teaspoon salt

Ingredients

Crispy Sesame Kale

Baking kale for just 10 minutes with a little bit of oil turns it into the most wonderfully fun, crispy side dish. Curly kale works best here. Oh, kale, is there anything you can't stand up to? Greens in the oven. Who knew?! This would be especially nice as a base for some roasted veggies and baked tofu, or you could sprinkle a tiny bit of seasoned rice vinegar over the top and eat it as a simple salad. Despite the Asian flavors, I think it'd go great with mashed potatoes and gravy, too.

Crispy Sesame Kale

Makes 2 to 4 servings

step 1 Preheat the oven to 375°F.

step 2 Tear the kale into bite-size pieces, then spread it out evenly on a cookie sheet covered in foil. Drizzle oil on top, then scrunch kale with your fingers until the oil is evenly distributed over the greens. Sprinkle the sesame seeds and salt over the top.

step 3 Bake in the oven for 10 minutes, until the leaves are crispy but still dark green. Serve.

Ingredients

1 head of kale, washed and deveined

1 tablespoon toasted sesame oil (the dark kind)

1 tablespoon sesame seeds

1 pinch to $\frac{1}{8}$ teaspoon salt (I originally tried this with $\frac{1}{4}$ teaspoon salt and it was way too salty. The kale will cook down in the oven, so you don't need as much salt as you might be tempted to add!)

Moroccan Spiced Root Vegetable Home Fries

If you're looking to jazz up your regular home fries, these will do the trick. The spice mix is easy to throw together but gives an impressive complexity to the dish without being overwhelming. It's also good for other dishes, too. You can use whatever combination of root veggies you want. I've used an equal ratio of potatoes, sweet potatoes, and celery root. If you're new to celery root, this is a great dish to try it in. I served these fries to a friend and she loved them. When she was done eating, I told her she just ate celeriac. Her response was, "I did? Way to go, me!"

Moroccan Spiced Root Vegetable Home Fries

Makes 2 to 3 servings

step 1 Heat the oil in a large, cast-iron sauté pan, as this will give the best browning and is also nonstick. Dice the potato, sweet potato, and celery root. The easiest way to do this is to make long, even vegetable sticks and then slice the sticks into even cubes.

step 2 Once the pan is hot enough to sizzle when the vegetables are added, add all of the cubed veggies. They should be in only one layer in the pan. However, take care that the pan isn't *too* hot, or the veggies will brown before they're fully cooked. Cook for several minutes, allowing to brown all over, turning to brown all the sides.

step 3 If the vegetables aren't quite soft enough yet but are as browned as you want them to be, add 2 tablespoons of water to the hot pan and cover immediately. Cook for 2 to 3 minutes. This will steam the vegetables and complete the cooking process.

step 4 Add the cumin, coriander, curry, cardamom, cinnamon, salt, and sugar and toss well, cooking for 1 minute more. Serve.

Ingredients

1 to 2 tablespoons olive oil

1 cup cubed potato

1 cup cubed sweet potato

1 cup cubed celery root

$1/4$ teaspoon cumin

$1/4$ teaspoon coriander

$1/4$ teaspoon curry powder, any kind

$1/4$ teaspoon cardamom

$1/4$ teaspoon cinnamon

$1/4$ teaspoon salt

$1/4$ teaspoon sugar

Pan-Seared Tomato and Rosemary Artichoke Sandwich

I hope I can unite two types of people with this sandwich: those who dislike fresh tomatoes and those who love them. I'll admit, I'm in the former group. Sometimes I can handle a sliced tomato on a sandwich, but I usually end up picking it out halfway through. The tomatoes in this sandwich are cooked quickly in a hot skillet. They're in there long enough to lose the raw flavor, but not so long you feel bad about cooking your perfectly vine-ripened tomatoes— and I do mean perfectly ripened. This sandwich showcases summer tomatoes in all their glory. If so-delicious-they-make-you-wanna-cry red and juicy tomatoes are not available, consider another sandwich. You make the call.

An optional but crazy-good addition to this sandwich is a balsamic reduction. If you've never made a balsamic reduction, you're in for a treat. Fancy restaurants use it all the freakin' time, but it only requires one ingredient: balsamic vinegar. It can be a little tricky, because if you reduce it too much it just tastes burned or it starts to caramelize and will be hard as a rock when it cools. But keep an eye on it and you'll be fine. It's the perfect thing to drizzle over lightly cooked summer veggies, so keep it in mind for other meals.

Vegan Yum Yum

Pan-Seared Tomato and Rosemary Artichoke Sandwich

Makes 1 sandwich

step 1 If using, make the balsamic vinegar reduction and set it aside. This can be made ahead of time.

step 2 Heat the oil in a sauté pan and add the rosemary and artichokes. Sprinkle with a pinch of salt and cook over medium heat for a few minutes until the edges start to turn golden. Don't worry if they break up a bit. Once cooked, remove to a small bowl.

step 3 Slice the tomato into $1/4$- to $1/2$-inch slices. You do not need to de-seed it unless it's a huge tomato and it's dripping with seeds. I leave the seeds in. You want the slices to be decently thick, as this will prevent them from falling apart completely in the pan.

step 4 Put the tomatoes into the same pan the artichokes were in (don't bother to wash it!), and cook 1 to 2 minutes on each side. You shouldn't need more oil; the liquid from the tomatoes will work just fine. Sprinkle each side with a pinch of salt and some pepper. You want to cook them long enough so they begin to soften and get juicy, but not so long that they fall apart. If they do fall apart, or a few slices do, no worries! Using a spatula, remove them from your pan to a plate.

Ingredients

Balsamic reduction, if using *(see recipe on page 98)*

1 tablespoon olive oil

$1/2$ teaspoon dried rosemary

2 artichoke hearts, canned *(packed in water)*, sliced

1 pinch salt

1 medium tomato, heart-breakingly ripe

2 pinches salt

Black pepper, to taste

2 slices sourdough bread *(from a larger round loaf or whatever bread you prefer)*

1 to 2 teaspoons olive oil, for drizzling on bread

Baby spinach and/or fresh basil

step 5 Drizzle the bread slices lightly with olive oil and grill them. (You can also just oil the grill or a pan and toast it that way.) I do this step last so the bread is still warm and toasty.

step 6 To assemble the sandwich, place the spinach or basil on one slice of the bread, and then the artichokes. Drizzle with the balsamic reduction if using. Top with tomatoes and place the other bread slice on top. You want the tomatoes to be next to one of the pieces of bread so it soaks up the yummy juices.

Picnic Sandwich

I make these when my husband, Stewart, and I travel, though admittedly on regular sandwich bread. If you wrap them up tightly in plastic wrap, they get all crazy delicious while you reach your destination. I usually make them for plane rides and other such occasions, but I have a fantasy of some lovely midsummer picnic that involves a few of these sandwiches. They're wonderful when eaten immediately, but this is definitely a sandwich that can withstand being tossed around in a backpack for a few hours before consuming. I fancied it up with a grilled baguette, but by all means, use regular toasted sandwich bread. That's how we usually eat them anyway! I use pine nuts because I'm addicted to them, but feel free to use a less expensive nut. You can also use part pine nuts and part some other nut to make the spread.

½ cup pine nuts, dry toasted *(or other nut of your choice)*

⅓ cup sun-dried tomatoes, oil packed

1 roasted red pepper *(jarred peppers work fine)*

1 zucchini

1 teaspoon *(or a little more)* olive oil

½ to 1 teaspoon Italian herbs, dried, your choice

Salt, to taste

Pepper, to taste

1 French baguette

1 cup baby spinach

Picnic Sandwich

Makes 2 large baguette sandwiches

step 1 Place the pine nuts in a dry skillet over medium heat. Toss occasionally; more often when nuts turn shiny. When browned on both sides, remove from the pan immediately. Be careful not to burn these—you don't want to leave the kitchen while toasting!

step 2 Place pine nuts and tomatoes in a food processor and blend until smooth (or however close to smooth you feel like getting). It can be chunky, too. The oil on the tomatoes is usually enough to make a nice spread consistency, but if you're using dry sundried tomatoes, add a drizzle of olive oil. Set aside.

step 3 If you're roasting the pepper, start that now. Jarred roasted peppers (water packed) work great too.

step 4 Chop the zucchini into rectangles ¼-inch thick. Heat 1 teaspoon or so of the olive oil in a sauté pan, just enough to coat the bottom. Turn the heat up to high and wait a minute or two for the pan to get very hot.

step 5 Place about ½ teaspoon of herbs in the bottom of the pan; they should sizzle. Add the zucchini rectangles in one layer, pressing down on them with a spatula. You want to cook them very quickly, browning them on both sides before they get too soft. Sprinkle with salt and pepper while in the pan and remove once each piece has some color on both sides.

step 6 To assemble the sandwich, toast or grill the bread. Spread each side generously with the pine nut and tomato mixture. Lay the zucchini down, followed by the roasted red pepper. (You can keep the pepper whole or slice it into strips.) Add baby spinach, press sandwich together, and serve or wrap tightly in plastic wrap or foil.

Salt and Pepper Potato Chips

If you have a mandoline or a vegetable slicer, you should absolutely make your own potato chips! They're fast, flavorful, and customizable—not to mention ridiculously tasty because they're so darn fresh. If you've got a sharp knife and skills to match, you can try slicing these out by hand, but it was impossible for me to do it without the help of a slicer. You can get small hand slicers with ceramic or metal blades that work well and are very inexpensive if you don't want to purchase a mandoline.

A quick word on potatoes: the type of spud matters. When you're frying a potato, you want to select a variety that has a high starch count and a low sugar count, like a russet potato. A waxier potato that has more sugar will brown before it crisps fully; the sugars will caramelize too soon, giving you the difficult choice between a soggy chip or a burned one. A starchy potato, on the other hand, can hold its own in the oil much better, and you'll end up with a delightfully crunchy, golden crisp.

Salt and Pepper Potato Chips

Makes 2 servings, easily scaled

step 1 In a large pan (a deep cast-iron skillet works well) heat the oil to 350°F.

step 2 Slice the potatoes very thinly (as seen in the photo), add them to the oil one at a time, and fry until golden and crispy, 30 seconds to 1 minute each. Remove them and drain on paper towels. While they are still hot and wet from the oil, sprinkle them with fresh-ground black pepper, sugar, and salt. Serve.

2 to 3 cups canola or peanut oil for frying

2 potatoes, scrubbed *(skins optional)*

1 teaspoon fresh ground black pepper

1 pinch sugar

3 pinches salt

Ingredients

Smoky Miso Tofu Sandwiches

hate it when I order a tofu sandwich somewhere and it pretty much tastes like (or actually is) blocks of watery, plain tofu stuffed between two pieces of bread. What's up with that? You might as well be eating a wet, mushy sponge. I love tofu, but you've got to treat it right, you know?

So I was thinking about tofu and imagining thin slices of flavorful goodness to stuff into sandwiches. I knew I wanted to use miso as the base for the flavor. The first sauce I mixed together used a bit of maple syrup, which seemed like a good idea until I tasted it. Something about the combination of red miso and maple syrup did not sit well with me, so down the drain it went. I moved on to pure, unadulterated sugar, a twist of lemon, and a splash of tamari. I was definitely getting close to what I had in mind. I scooped in a little bit of nooch (nutritional yeast, aka vegan pixie dust) and Liquid Smoke and it was finished. It's a dead-simple marinade: tangy, salty, smoky, and rich. I wanted to eat it like a soup. This tofu keeps well, so it's nice to make a whole block and set it aside for sandwiches, salads, or snacking directly out of the fridge.

Smoky Miso
Tofu Sandwiches

Makes 18 to 20 thin slices, for 4 to 5 sandwiches

step 1 Preheat the oven to 425°F. Wrap your drained tofu in a few paper towels, then again in a terry cloth bar towel. Press with something heavy, like a cast-iron skillet or a plate with some cans on top, for 10 to 20 minutes.

step 2 Meanwhile, mix together the miso, lemon juice, sugar, tamari, yeast, and Liquid Smoke to make a marinade.

step 3 Unwrap the tofu and cut many thin, width-wise slices with a large knife (I got 18 to 20 slices out of one block of tofu).

step 4 Line up your tofu slices on a baking sheet that is covered with parchment paper or a Silpat baking

1 block extra-super-firm tofu, drained and pressed

3 tablespoons red miso

3 tablespoons lemon juice

3 tablespoons sugar

3 tablespoons tamari or soy sauce

1 tablespoon nutritional yeast

1/4 teaspoon Liquid Smoke flavoring

Ingredients

mat. Brush both sides of the tofu with the marinade.

step 5 Let the slices absorb the marinade for 10 minutes or so, then brush just the tops again. Bake for 20 minutes. Remove from the oven and let the slices cool on the sheet. The tofu should be darkened around the edges, but not burned.

step 6 To make a sandwich using the tofu slices, use whatever sandwich ingredients you love. I'm a simple girl, so some vegan mayo, baby spinach, and sourdough toast were all I needed to make a delicious sandwich. Most likely, whatever your favorite

sandwich fixings are, they will go great with this tofu. This also makes a great vegan BLT! You can refrigerate the remaining slices to use later.

Three-Spice Potatoes

Oven-roasted potatoes need little embellishment. These potatoes are roasted with three spices—cumin, coriander, and mustard seeds—giving them a flavor that doesn't overwhelm. A little bit of lemon finishes them; I guarantee you'll want seconds!

3 medium-size Yukon Gold potatoes *(about 15 ounces)*

3 tablespoons vegetable oil

1 teaspoon cumin seeds

1 teaspoon black or brown mustard seeds

1/2 teaspoon coriander powder

1/4 teaspoon salt

1 tablespoon fresh lemon juice, plus extra for seasoning

Salt, to taste for seasoning

Pepper, to taste for seasoning

Three-Spice Potatoes

Makes 2 servings

step 1   Preheat the oven to 400°F.

step 2   Scrub potatoes and leave the skins on. Cut the potatoes in half lengthwise, then in half lengthwise again to form four long wedges. Cut each wedge in half to form thin, wedgelike "oven fries."

step 3   Heat the oil in a large oven-proof skillet with a tight-fitting lid. Add the cumin seeds, mustard seeds, coriander powder, and salt to the skillet and mix well, until the seeds begin to pop, and then add the lemon juice. When the bubbling subsides, add the potatoes and toss well to coat with the oil and spices. Make sure the potatoes are resting on their cut sides (as opposed to their skins). Cover and place in the oven for 20 minutes.

step 4   Remove the pan from the oven and use a spatula to loosen the potatoes from the bottom of the pan. Turn them so the browned sides are up and place them back in the oven for another 10 to 15 minutes, uncovered, or until potatoes are tender but still hold their shape.

step 5   Finish the potatoes under the broiler to give a perfect oven-roasted color to the potatoes if needed. When finished baking, squeeze a bit of extra lemon juice and a dash of salt over the top. Serve immediately.

chapter six

Soups

African Yam Stew

This soup is hot, spicy, and sort of sweet. Fresh, whole spices really give this soup a lot of kick, so if you don't have any on hand, consider buying some. They'll stay fresh for one to two years if tightly covered, and your cooking will be even more awesome when you use them. If you know you don't like spicy-hot, ease up on the pepper flakes and ginger. That being said, this soup isn't crazy hot, so give it a whirl as is! I love the textures in this—the creamy yams (well, they're technically sweet potatoes, but whatever), the plump, juicy raisins, the tender kale. I used a mortar and pestle to grind my spices, but feel free to use a spice grinder.

African Yam Stew

Makes 4 to 5 servings

step 1 Grind the cumin, peppercorns, coriander seeds, red pepper flakes, mustard seeds, and whole cloves in a spice grinder (or crush in a mortar and pestle) and set aside.

step 2 Heat the vegetable oil in a large, heavy-bottomed pot with a tight-fitting lid. Add the onions and cook on medium-low until they begin to caramelize.

step 3 Meanwhile, prepare the yam, kale, and carrots. Once the veggies are prepped, dump your spice mixture into the oil and cook for 1 minute, being careful not to burn. Stop the cooking by dumping in the tomatoes and their juices, yams, kale and carrots. Then add the water, raisins, peanut butter, ginger, and salt and bring to a rolling boil. Turn down the heat and cover. Cook for 30 to 40 minutes, or until the yams and carrots are tender and the raisins are nice and plump. Serve.

1/2 teaspoon cumin seeds

1/2 teaspoon peppercorns

1/2 teaspoon coriander seeds

1/2 teaspoon red pepper flakes

1/2 teaspoon mustard seeds

2 whole cloves

1 to 2 tablespoons vegetable oil

1 small onion, finely chopped

1 garnet yam, softball-size, peeled and cut into 1/2-inch chunks *(may substitute jewel yams)*

1 bunch kale, deveined and shredded

3 small carrots, peeled and sliced into coins

1 13.5-ounce can stewed tomatoes, blended smooth if you like

4 cups water

1/2 cup raisins

1/2 cup peanut butter *(optional; pictured without)*

Fresh ginger, 1-to 2-inch piece, peeled and grated*

1/2 teaspoon kosher salt

*Note: Peel the ginger with a vegetable peeler and grate it, using a circular motion, on the second-to-smallest holes on your grater. You should end up with nice, juicy pulp on the inside of the grater and a mass of fibers in your hand. Discard the fibers and use the pulp in the soup.

Basic Vegetable Soup

This is a great basic minestrone-style soup. You can play with the ingredients to use what you have on hand, making it a good "clean out the fridge" soup, too.

Basic Vegetable Soup

Makes 6 servings

step 1 Heat the oil over medium-high heat in a large pot with a lid. Add the onion and sauté until soft and beginning to color. Add the garlic and sauté for another few seconds, until fragrant. Add the potatoes, carrots, celery salt, sage, oregano, and rosemary and cook until very fragrant, for another 2 to 3 minutes.

step 2 Add the water, bouillon cubes, tomato paste, and pasta and stir well. Bring to a boil and stir until the tomato paste is dissolved. Cook, covered, gently boiling, for 10 minutes.

step 3 Add the greens, corn, lemon juice, salt, and black pepper. Adjust the seasonings to taste and cook until the pasta is done and the carrots and potatoes are cooked through but not overly mushy. Serve.

Ingredients

1 to 2 tablespoons vegetable oil, your choice

1 medium sweet onion, minced

4 cloves garlic, minced *(optional)*

3 cups red potato, cut into small chunks

$1\frac{1}{2}$ cups carrot, sliced into coins and then roughly chopped

$\frac{1}{4}$ teaspoon celery salt

$\frac{1}{2}$ teaspoon sage

$\frac{1}{2}$ teaspoon oregano

$\frac{1}{2}$ teaspoon rosemary

7 cups water

2 vegetable bouillon cubes

$\frac{1}{4}$ cup tomato paste

1 cup elbow macaroni *(or other small pasta shape)*

2 cups packed greens *(like kale, chard, collards, etc., torn into bite-sized pieces)*

2 ears corn *(about $\frac{2}{3}$ cup)*

2 tablespoons lemon juice, fresh

$\frac{1}{2}$ teaspoon salt

Black pepper, to taste

Black Bean Soup

I love black beans. I especially love them with coconut milk in soups. The coconut milk is optional here, but it's oh-so-delicious. It's hard to tell, but in these pictures, one soup has the coconut milk in it and the other does not. You stir it in just before you serve it, so feel free to ask the preference of your guest. It's easy to make some bowls with and some bowls without. This soup starts with a mirepoix, which is a classic combination of onions, celery, and carrots, all of which are known as aromatics. Traditionally, the ratio for mirepoix is 2:1:1 onions, carrots, celery. This soup is closer to 1:1:1, but it's very flexible. Feel free to alter the ratio. I also haven't called for the mirepoix to be uniformly diced, as I don't think it makes a difference in this soup. However, feel free to be uniform with your dicing if you're feeling fancy and have some time to kill with your chef's knife.

Black Bean Soup

Makes 2 servings

step 1 Heat the oil in a large, heavy-bottomed pot over medium heat. Add the onions and cook for 1 minute. Add the carrots and cook for 3 minutes. Add the celery and cook for 2 minutes. Add the red pepper, thyme, cumin, black pepper, beans, tomatoes, salt, and tamari and stir well.

step 2 Cover and let the ingredients cook for 5 minutes. Remove cover, stir, and let simmer for an additional 5 minutes. Taste for seasoning and add more salt, if needed. Turn off the heat and stir in the coconut milk. Serve immediately, topped with fresh red bell pepper and a celery leaf for garnish.

1 to 2 tablespoons vegetable oil, your choice

¼ cup minced onion

1 medium carrot, sliced into thin coins

2 small ribs of celery, chopped (*¼ cup total; reserve leaves for garnish*)

¼ cup diced red pepper

½ teaspoon thyme

¼ teaspoon cumin

Black pepper, to taste

1 14-ounce can black beans, undrained

1 cup tomatoes blended (*if fresh, about 3 small tomatoes*) or 1 cup canned diced

½ teaspoon salt

1 tablespoon low-sodium tamari

¼ cup coconut milk (*optional, but recommended*)

Diced red pepper, for garnish

Cannellini Bean Soup with Pan-fried Croutons

I created this soup after I had a similar one in a restaurant in my neighborhood. I couldn't stop thinking about it, so I deconstructed it and recreated it in my own kitchen. It's very simple and fresh, but bursting with flavor. Crispy fried croutons pair perfectly with soft beans and tender kale, while little grape tomatoes give bursts of sweetness. This is definitely one of my all-time favorite soups, and you can prepare the croutons for any other recipe you like.

Cannellini Bean Soup with Pan-fried Croutons

Makes 2 servings

step 1 To make the pan-fried croutons, melt the margarine in a skillet and add the bread cubes. Let the bread fry, absorbing the margarine, until golden brown. Toss to brown all sides of the croutons and remove from the pan when they are rich brown and crispy. Set aside.

step 2 Heat the olive oil in a soup pot. Add the shallots and sauté until tender and lightly colored. Pour in the vegetable stock and heat until simmering. Add the kale, beans, and salt and cook, covered, until the kale is tender but still dark green.

step 3 When ready to serve, turn off the heat and add the tomatoes. Let them sit in the hot soup for 1 to 3 minutes to cook slightly before serving. Check the seasoning and adjust, if desired. Add the pan-fried croutons at the last moment, with a small squeeze of lemon juice, if desired.

Ingredients

2 tablespoons Earth Balance margarine

3 slices whole wheat bread, sliced into $1/4$-inch cubes

2 tablespoons extra virgin olive oil

2 to 3 shallots, peeled and sliced

4 cups Homemade Vegetable Stock *(see recipe on page 176)*

2 to 3 kale leaves, torn

1 14-ounce can cannelinni beans, drained

$1/2$ to 1 teaspoon salt

16 grape tomatoes, halved

fresh lemon juice, for seasoning

Chinese Broccoli Wontons in a Ginger-Soy Broth

This isn't a traditional wonton soup. I suppose a vegan wonton soup wouldn't really be considered traditional anyway, but I really took some liberty with the recipe. The wontons are stuffed with one of my favorite greens, Chinese broccoli, and chopped seitan. I tossed the filling in a chili-mustard sauce for a salty, spicy kick. The slight bitterness of the Chinese broccoli really balances the piquant heat of the dressing, creating a really yummy dumpling.

I wanted the wontons to be the star here, so I made a very light ginger-soy broth to float them in. I only covered the wontons about halfway with the soup base, so really, this isn't so much a soup as fresh dumplings lightly dressed with an aromatic broth. In fact, the broth is quite plain on its own, but it works very nicely with the flavorful dumplings.

Chinese broccoli is fantastic, and if you've never had it, I wholly recommend a search of your nearest Asian grocer to find some. It's a vegetable chimera of all of my favorite things: the florets of broccoli

Vegan Yum Yum

rabe, the stems of asparagus, and leaves like tender collard greens. It has a mild flavor with a sweet and slightly bitter bite, and it's perfect for stir-fries or any other high-heat/quick-cooking method. It's also quite good for you, and its complex flavor is a nice change of pace from regular broccoli or simple spinach.

Folding wontons isn't hard—as long as you can find the wonton skins, you'll be good to go. The brand I used here is called Twin Marquis, and they make both vegan and nonvegan wonton skins and gyoza wrappers. Look for the white (not yellow) square wrappers. The round ones are gyoza skins, much better for pot stickers; even though they're similar, they're a good deal thicker than the wonton skins. Either way, check the label for eggs.

If you have leftover wonton skins, you can make extra wontons and freeze them in one layer on a cookie sheet, then transfer them to a freezer bag for long-term storage. Just drop them directly into boiling water when you're ready to cook them. You can also wrap the skins up tightly and store them in the fridge for a day or two. Fill them with anything you like (spinach and Tofutti cream cheese? Tempeh sausage?), fold in half, and seal shut. Panfry them in 1 to 2 inches of oil until crispy and golden brown. It's a wonderfully tasty and quick appetizer or snack.

1 cup Chinese broccoli, sliced thin

1 tablespoon oil

1 to 2 teaspoons fresh ginger, minced

3/4 cup seitan, chopped fine

1/2 teaspoon hot chili sauce, more if desired *(like Sriracha)*

1 teaspoon Dijon mustard

2 tablespoons plus 1 teaspoon tamari *(or soy sauce)*

4 cups water

5 to 6 fresh ginger slices

1 tablespoon mirin

1 1/2 teaspoons sugar

2 teaspoons rice vinegar

1/2 teaspoon salt, plus more to taste

1/4 cup Chinese broccoli leaves, packed *(or substitute spinach or collards)*

16 wonton skins

Chinese Broccoli Wontons in a Ginger-Soy Broth

Makes 4 servings

step 1 Begin by chopping the Chinese broccoli very thin with a sharp knife, from the base of the stem up toward the leaves (just like chopping scallions). Heat the oil in a large pan and add the ginger. Once the ginger becomes fragrant, add the broccoli and seitan, stirring well and cooking until the broccoli is bright green and tender-crisp.

step 2 Transfer the broccoli-seitan filling to a small bowl and toss with the chili sauce, mustard, and 1 teaspoon of tamari (or soy sauce). Taste and adjust to your liking. Set aside while you make the broth.

step 3 To make the broth, in a small saucepan, heat the water, ginger slices, mirin, remaining tamari (or soy sauce), sugar, rice vinegar, and salt until the sugar and salt are dissolved and the ginger has had time to infuse the broth. Taste and add more salt if desired, but remember: this is a mild broth that is only meant to be a complement to the wontons. Once the broth has begun to simmer, turn off the heat and toss in the Chinese broccoli leaves (or your choice of greens). Cover and set aside.

step 4 To fill the wontons, place 1 to 2 teaspoons of the broccoli-seitan filling in the center of the wonton. Wet the edges of the wrapper with water (a finger dipped in water works great) and seal into a triangle, removing as much air as possible from the dumpling. Make sure the edges are secure.

step 5 Set the triangle in front of you, pointing up. Wet one of the bottom corners. Hold the corners, one between each thumb and forefinger. Begin to bend the wrapper, as if you were forcing it into a horseshoe shape. Don't change your grip, and resist the urge to fold the corners over. Bring the two ends together, crossing them slightly, and press to seal. Going from the triangle shape to a completed wonton is one fluid motion.

step 6 Your dumpling should look like a fun little fish-boat-hat.

step 7 You can now freeze your dumplings or cook them right away.

step 8 To prepare the soup, bring a pot of salted water to a boil. Reheat your broth to steaming, if necessary. Gently lower the wontons into the boiling water and cook until they become translucent, about 2 to 3 minutes if the wontons aren't frozen, longer if they are. Remove them from the water with a spider (or other slotted spoon device) and place them into the hot broth.

step 9 Take care to remove and discard any dumplings that have opened up during cooking. If they open, water gets inside, washes all the flavor away, and you'll be sad if you serve it or eat it. It will taste like watery mush, and I promise you won't be happy about it.

step 10 Ladle 3 to 4 wontons into a bowl and add a small amount of broth, enough to halfway cover the wontons. Make sure to get some greens in there, too. Serve immediately.

Chipotle Basil Corn Chowder

This soup has a kick to it, and it's a great way to use up summer produce. The soup pictured here used the corn, basil, potatoes, onions, and carrots that I got in my CSA share one week. Fresh corn will give the best results, but you can try frozen if it's all you've got; just be sure to rinse it under cool water before adding it to the soup to remove any weird freezer taste. If you're opening a new can of chipotle in adobo, freeze the rest for later use.

1 tablespoon olive oil

1 small onion, finely diced (*1/2 cup*)

5 small red potatoes, diced small (*3 cups*)

1 cup shredded carrot

1 teaspoon chipotle in adobo, minced (*canned*)

3 cups water

1 vegetable bouillon cube

3 cups fresh sweet corn (*5 to 6 ears*), divided

1/2 cup soy milk

1/2 teaspoon salt

1 tablespoon lime juice

1/2 cup fresh basil, chopped

Fresh black pepper, to taste

Chipotle Basil Corn Chowder

Makes 4 servings

step 1 Heat the olive oil in a large pot with a tight-fitting lid. Add the onions and sauté until golden. Add the potatoes, carrot, and chipotle and stir to coat. Let them cook over medium heat for a minute, and don't worry if they start to stick.

step 2 Add the water and bouillon cube and mix well, scraping what's sticking off the bottom of the pan. Bring to a boil, then reduce heat and cover, cooking for 10 minutes or until potatoes are tender.

step 3 Transfer all or half of the mixture to a blender (only transfer 1/2 if you want some potato chunks in the finished product). Add half of the corn, soy milk, salt, and lime juice and blend until smooth. Return to the pot and stir in most of the basil (keep out a few of the basil leaves for garnish) and black pepper to taste. Taste and add additional seasoning if necessary.

step 4 Ladle the soup into bowls and distribute the remaining corn over the top. Garnish with fresh black pepper and a few small basil leaves. Serve immediately.

Creamy Broccoli Dal

ed lentil dal and cream of broccoli soup got together and had a love child. This is a mild Indian-spiced soup with all the comforts of standard cream of broccoli. If you want to make a bigger batch, it doubles well. It's easy to make, too!

1 to 2 tablespoons vegetable oil, your choice

1 teaspoon cumin seeds

1 teaspoon mustard seeds (black)

¼ cup onion, finely chopped

½ cup red lentils (masoor dal)

1 whole broccoli stalk, peeled and finely chopped (just over 2-plus cups, packed)*

2 cups water

½ teaspoon salt

1 cup soy milk

1 tablespoon soy sauce (or salt to taste)

1 tablespoon lemon juice

½ teaspoon turmeric

½ teaspoon garam masala

½ teaspoon red pepper flakes (optional)

Salt, to taste, if needed

*Note: Trim off the bottom 1 to 2 inches of the stalk to remove the tough part, but use the tender parts of the stalk and the florets in this recipe. Peeling them with a vegetable peeler will remove any fibrous qualities of the stalk, but it's not necessary. You can chop the broccoli by hand, or cut it up into chucks and pulse them in your food processor until well chopped.

Creamy Broccoli Dal

Makes 2 servings

step 1 Heat the oil on medium-high to high in a 2- to 3-quart pot. Add the cumin and mustard seeds, onion, and lentils. Fry in the oil until the seeds are popping and the lentils have changed color slightly, being careful not to burn them. The onions should be soft and maybe even getting some color.

step 2 Add the broccoli, water, and salt. Bring to a boil, then cover and simmer for 20 to 25 minutes, stirring every once in a while. At this point, the soup should be thick but still watery, and the broccoli should be soft.

step 3 Add the soy milk, soy sauce, lemon juice, turmeric, garam masala, red pepper flakes, and salt and turn down the heat; you don't want to boil the soup anymore or the soy milk might start to look funny. Stir well and adjust the seasoning if needed. Serve immediately.

Homemade Vegetable Stock

Making your own vegetable stock is wonderfully easy and blissfully imprecise. There is only 20 minutes of active time, it doesn't really require a recipe, it uses up those veggies in your fridge you've been meaning to eat, it tastes great, it stores easily, and is highly customizable. If you're part of a CSA and the fall harvest of veggies has you overwhelmed, simply put the veggies you can't figure out how to eat in your broth. I would say there are only three required vegetables for your stock: onions, carrots, and celery.

Onions, carrots, and celery are known collectively as mirepoix, a classic part of French cuisine. All of these vegetables are aromatics, and you'll realize that as soon as you start cooking them together; suddenly your kitchen smells like Thanksgiving. You can fancy it up a bit if you feel like it by using parsnips instead of carrots, leeks instead of onions, or celeriac instead of celery. Mirepoix is a great culinary trick to keep up your sleeve; it's a great starting point for many, many recipes, especially soups and sauces. It's not called the holy trinity of French cuisine for nothing.

Minimalist Broth:

2 to 3 tablespoons olive oil

1 to 2 large onions, chopped

1 pound celery, chopped

1 pound carrots, washed but unpeeled, chopped

3 whole cloves garlic

1 bay leaf

10 whole black peppercorns

2 teaspoon salt

¼ cup low-sodium tamari

1 gallon water

You might also have or want to use any of the following:

Celery root
Mushrooms
Turnips
Fennel
Parsnips
Veggie scraps from other meals
Fresh herbs
Peppers
Zucchini
Greens (any)
Potatoes
Leeks
Tomato paste

Homemade Vegetable Stock

Makes 10 cups of broth

If it's clean and fits in the pot, it can go in. Minimal chopping, no peeling—just in the pot it goes!

step 1 Heat a large stockpot with some olive oil in the bottom. I chop my way through the vegetable list as I'm cooking, so once the onion is chopped, I add it to the pot, then do the celery, the carrots, and so on, adding each thing once it's chopped up a bit. When you're out of stuff to add, pour in the water, turn up the heat, and cover. It should only take you about 20 minutes to chop everything and get it in the pot. From then on, it's easy street.

Vegan Yum Yum

step 2 Cook for 1 hour, turning the heat down a bit once the whole thing starts boiling.

step 3 I finish my stock by adding salt/tamari/soy sauce to taste and letting it simmer uncovered for another 20 to 30 minutes to concentrate the flavors.

step 4 Strain the veggies through a sieve into a large pot. I further strain it through cheesecloth into a pitcher. The pitcher makes it easy to pour some of the stock into ice cube trays for easy storage. Ice cube– size chunks of stock make for easy defrosting and easy recipe additions.

step 5 The stock will keep for about a week in your refrigerator, and two good months in your freezer. If you cook for the holidays, make it and freeze it a few weeks before. You'll thank yourself for being prepared, and your food will be that much more delectable!

Potato Leek Soup

This is the perfect soup with which to welcome the fall, when leeks and potatoes are in season and at their most flavorful. If you use a really nice vegetable broth as the base, you'll be surprised how rich the soup can be even with so few ingredients.

Vegan Yum Yum

Potato Leek Soup

Makes 3-4 servings

step 1 Remove tough leaves from the leek bulbs and discard them. Slice the long, white/pale green bulbs in half lengthwise and run under cool water, being careful to remove any dirt or sand that may be trapped between the layers. Thinly slice the leeks crosswise.

step 2 Heat the oil in a soup pot and add the garlic. Sauté for 1 minute and then add the leeks. Stir well. Cook the leeks until tender, about 2 to 3 minutes.

step 3 Add the potatoes and broth along with the salt and bay leaf. Boil, covered, until the potatoes are very tender and almost falling apart.

step 4 Blend the soup in a blender or food processor while it's still hot, in batches if necessary. Return the soup to the pot and reheat if necessary, seasoning with pepper and more salt, if needed. Serve.

Ingredients

3 cups leeks, thinly sliced *(2 to 3 leeks)*

3 tablespoons olive oil

3 cloves garlic, peeled and pressed

1 pound potatoes, peeled and cubed

4 cups Homemade Vegetable Broth *(see recipe on page 176)*

1 teaspoon salt

1 bay leaf

1 to 2 teaspoons fresh black pepper, to taste

Spicy Tomato Chickpea Soup

Looking for a nice tomato soup to sip, but want something with a little punch? This soup has chickpeas blended right in. They not only give the soup extra body and flavor, but also pack in some protein, iron, and fiber. I like to blend the whole soup and serve it in mugs, but you can also blend only half and have some chickpea and tomato chunks in your finished soup. It's wonderful with toast!

Spicy Tomato Chickpea Soup

Makes 4 servings

step 1 Heat the oil in a large skillet with high sides. Add the onion and sauté for 2 to 3 minutes until softened. Add the garlic, cumin, and chili flakes and stir for another minute.

step 2 Add the mustard seeds, turmeric, and the drained chickpeas. Sauté until the chickpeas begin to turn golden.

step 3 Add the tomatoes and salt and let simmer for 10 to 15 minutes until the tomatoes are cooked.

step 4 Transfer the mixture—all or half of it—to a blender. Add the nutritional yeast and hot water and blend until smooth. Blend in batches if you can't fit everything at the same time. Taste and add more salt if needed. Serve with fresh cracked black pepper.

Ingredients

2 to 3 tablespoons vegetable oil, your choice

1 sweet onion

2 to 3 cloves garlic, minced *(optional)*

1/2 teaspoon cumin

1/2 teaspoon chili flakes

1/2 teaspoon mustard seeds

1/2 teaspoon turmeric

1 15-ounce can chickpeas, drained and rinsed

1 28-ounce can diced tomatoes

1 teaspoon salt

2 tablespoons nutritional yeast *(optional)*

1 cup hot water

Black pepper, to taste

Tanuki Soba with Spinach Tempura

Tanuki soba is a noodle soup in a soy/miso broth that is topped with fried tempura batter. Tanuki is a character in Japanese folklore, a raccoon dog who is both mischievous and jolly. The soup is named after him because the fried tempura batter, floating on top of the soup (see last photo), looks as though it is more filling and nutritious than it really is—it doesn't contain vegetables or anything substantial, just soft, fried batter, another one of Tanuki's tricks. Nevertheless, I decided to add some baby spinach leaves to the batter. Sorry Tanuki! Feel free to use the tempura batter for standard tempura as well, even if you're not making this soup.

Tanuki Soba with Spinach Tempura

Yields: Makes 4 servings

step 1 Put some salted water on to boil for your noodles.

step 2 In a medium-size pot, make the broth by mixing together the water, sugar, tamari, and kombu, if using. Bring to a boil, then turn off the heat. Remove and discard the kombu, if using.

step 2 Place the miso into a bowl or a 2-cup measuring cup and add some of the hot soup broth. Mix until dissolved, then add back to the pot. Taste, adding more miso, tamari, or sugar to suit your taste. Cover broth and set aside. (If you reheat broth, be careful *not* to boil it again once the miso is added, as the delicate flavor of the miso will change if boiled.)

step 3 Add enough high-heat oil to a large skillet or wok until it is about $1/2$-inch deep. Heat the oil to medium-high (to about 375°F).

step 4 Boil the noodles, drain, rinse in cold water, and divide them between four bowls. Set aside.

step 5 Prepare the scallions and/or shredded carrot for garnishes and set aside.

step 6 Make the tempura batter by mixing together the egg replacer, water, and flour. Test the readiness of the oil by dribbling a little of the batter into it. The batter should bubble up immediately, but not turn brown. After a few minutes of cooking, it should be light and crispy.

Ingredients

1 package dried soba noodles *(250 grams/8.8 ounces)*

Broth *(see recipe below)*

High-heat oil *(like canola or peanut; amount will vary depending on what size pan you're using to fry the tempura batter in)*

Scallions and/or shredded carrot for garnishing

Tempura batter *(see recipe below)*

1 cup baby spinach

Broth:

4 cups water

1 tablespoon sugar

$1/3$ cup plus 1 tablespoon low-sodium tamari *(or soy sauce)*

1 x 2-inch piece of dried kombu seaweed *(optional but recommended)*

2 to 3 tablespoons miso *(I use sweet white, but use whatever you have)*

Tempura Batter:

1 tablespoon Ener-G Egg Replacer plus 3 tablespoons water

1 cup cold water

1 cup all-purpose flour

1 pinch salt

step 7 When the oil is ready, dip the spinach leaves individually into the tempura batter and then slide them into the oil. Try to keep them separate, but if a few stick together, that's fine. Do not overload the pan. After 30 seconds to 1 minute, use tongs to gently flip them. If you do this too early, the batter won't be set yet, and you'll smoosh the spinach. If you want, sprinkle some extra batter into the oil. Fry on the other side for one minute more, then remove to a paper towel with tongs or a slotted spoon.

step 8 Cover the noodles in the bowls with hot broth until they are almost completely submerged, but some still break through the surface. Add fried tempura drippings over the top of the soup, then pile the tempura spinach leaves in the middle. Sprinkle with garnishes and serve immediately.

Velvety Vegetable Soup

This soup is so comforting. It's like a big vegetable hug. It has a nice depth of flavor even though it really doesn't have that many vegetables in it. I wanted it to be a creamy minestrone type soup—you can see in the photos that I added white beans, whole carrots, and greens—but I wasn't too pleased with how it meshed with the base. Honestly, I love the smooth, velvety soup by itself. This is the recipe for the soup base only. Feel free to add veggies or cooked pasta, rice, whatever to the soup if you want. Otherwise just make the impossibly smooth soup and drink it from a coffee mug on a rainy day while watching an old movie. This soup works best in a high-speed blender, such as a Vita-Mix.

1 large sweet onion

1 tablespoon olive oil *(or vegetable oil of your choice)*

2 small carrots, peeled and chopped into thin rounds

7 cremini mushrooms, brushed, de-stemmed, and sliced

2 cloves garlic, chopped

1 13.5-ounce can stewed tomatoes

1¼ cans water *(use the tomato can)*

¼ teaspoon celery salt

¼ teaspoon paprika

1½ teaspoons kosher salt

½ teaspoon dried herbs *(your choice, but basil, oregano, and marjoram work well)*

½ teaspoon cumin

Black pepper, to taste

Optional mix-ins:

Cooked pasta, baby spinach, cooked barley, or your favorite mixed veggies

Velvety Vegetable Soup

Makes 4 servings

step 1 Cut the onion in half lengthwise. Trim off the ends, remove the skin, and make width-wise cuts to form onion half-moons. These will break apart into long strips.

step 2 Heat a heavy-bottomed skillet with the olive oil. Add the onions and sauté over medium heat until beginning to color. Add the carrots and mushrooms and cook down until the onions and mushrooms are very soft and the carrots have begun to soften. Add the garlic and sauté until fragrant and softened.

step 3 Add the cooked vegetables and the tomatoes, water, celery salt, paprika, kosher salt, dried herbs, cumin, and black pepper to your Vita-Mix, blender, or food processor. Process on high for as long as it takes to get the soup smooth. If using a Vita-Mix, process for 4 to 6 minutes or until soup is steaming hot and serve. For blenders and food processors, remove the soup and strain if necessary. Add to the soup pot and heat gently until hot enough to serve. Serve with a large chunk of toasted sourdough or your favorite bread.

chapter seven

Pasta

Baked Mac and Cheeze

People are picky about their nutritional yeast sauces, so I figure the more recipes out there for people to try, the better. This is a mild one. I think it would be especially great for kids, but my husband and I like it a lot. It makes a divine baked mac and cheeze, but you can pour it over pasta without baking it, use it on baked potatoes, or with your favorite veggies.

Go ahead and examine your soup bowls. A lot of bowls are labeled "oven safe" on the bottom, making them perfect for individual baked casseroles, like mac and cheeze, or even baked soups. This recipe will work in a larger casserole dish, too, but who wouldn't prefer their own bowl baked to perfection?

Baked Mac and Cheeze

Makes 4 servings

step 1 Preheat the oven to 400°F.

step 2 Cook the noodles and prepare the cheezy sauce.

step 3 Once the pasta is cooked and drained, toss with the prepared sauce and distribute into individual bowls.

step 4 Place bowls on a cookie sheet for easier handling. Top with bread crumbs and place the cookie sheet into the oven and bake for 20 to 25 minutes until bubbly. If needed, place under the broiler for 1 minute or more to brown top.

Cheezy Sauce

step 1 Melt the margarine in a saucepan over medium-low heat (be careful it's not too hot!). Once the margarine is melted, add the flour and whisk (you actually need a whisk for this) until dissolved, forming a roux.

step 2 Add the miso, tahini, tomato paste, soy sauce, and lemon juice. Whisk well (the mixture should be sort of thick).

step 3 Slowly whisk in the soy milk, making sure you don't have a pasty buildup on the sides of the pot. Turn the heat up a bit. Add the yeast, salt, and pepper and whisk until it thickens. Once it starts to boil, it should be sufficiently thick.

3 cups elbow macaroni

1 recipe Cheezy Sauce (see recipe below)

1 cup bread crumbs

Four oven-safe bowls or one casserole dish

Cheezy Sauce

Makes enough for 3 to 4 servings of pasta or rice

$1/3$ cup Earth Balance margarine

$1/4$ cup all-purpose flour

1 tablespoon miso, any flavor (I like red)

1 tablespoon tahini

1 tablespoon tomato paste

3 tablespoons low-sodium soy sauce or tamari

1 tablespoon lemon juice

$1 1/4$ cups soy milk

$1/3$ cup nutritional yeast

1 to 2 pinches salt, to taste, if needed

Black pepper, to taste

Gnocchi with Thyme Vinaigrette and Lemon Cashew Cream

In Italy, gnocchi doesn't require potatoes. Gnocchi can be made from regular pasta flour or cheese. In fact, pretty much anything that can be rolled into a lump and served like dumplings can be gnocchi. In the United States, however, gnocchi is usually assumed to be made mostly from potatoes. When it comes to potato gnocchi, there's a great debate between those who insist on adding eggs to the dough and those who insist that eggless gnocchi is the best. Being vegan, this is a problem easily solved. No eggs! There, that was easy, right?

Don't let anyone make you put eggs in your gnocchi! The downside is that eggless gnocchi can be a bit fussier than the egged version. But don't despair! I did a bunch of research, and I have a solid recipe here that will minimize, if not eliminate, any problems. These tips will be detailed in the recipe to follow.

Gnocchi with Thyme Vinaigrette and Lemon Cashew Cream

Makes 2 to 3 servings

step 1 Preheat the oven to 400°F. Stab your potatoes with a fork and wrap them in foil. Bake in a small dish for about 60 minutes, or until tender all the way through. Baked potatoes will be drier than boiled, so even though it takes longer, it makes for better gnocchi.

step 2 Put a large pot of salty water on to boil. It's important that you salt the water and not the dough; this will help keep the gnocchi firm. Salt is hygroscopic, meaning it absorbs water—salt in the dough would make your gnocchi a little mushy.

step 3 While the potatoes are baking and the water is heating up, build your workstation. You'll need the following: 1 knife (a paring knife is ideal), a fork or a gnocchi board, a large plate lightly dusted with flour (for shaping the gnocchi), and a large, flat surface for rolling out your pasta. A potato ricer (or a food mill) is ideal for ricing the potatoes, but a box grater or even just a fork will suffice. (For those who have never used a potato ricer, it's a common kitchen tool that pushes whole, cooked potatoes through a grate to make perfectly lumpless mashed potatoes [see the photos]).

step 5 Make the thyme vinaigrette by stripping the thyme leaves off of their stems into a mortar. Add a pinch or two of salt and grind with a pestle until a rough paste is formed. Add oil and vinegar and mix

Gnocchi

2 russet potatoes *(about 1½ pounds)*

1 scant cup bread flour *(I call for bread flour because of the high-gluten content. This will help the pasta set up while it's cooking a little better than regular flour would)*

(No salt!)

Thyme Vinaigrette

2 tablespoons fresh thyme, leaves only

1 to 2 pinches salt, to taste

¼ cup olive oil

1 teaspoon white wine vinegar

Lemon Cashew Cream

1 cup water

1¼ cups roasted, salted cashews *(or raw cashews)*

Zest of 1 lemon

½ to 1 teaspoon lemon juice

again. Don't worry if it's emulsified; it just needs to be mixed. Taste and adjust salt or vinegar as needed. Set aside.

step 8 To make the lemon cashew cream sauce, mix the water, roasted cashews, lemon zest, and lemon juice in a blender and blend on high until thick and smooth. Adjust seasoning if needed (this should taste slightly sweet and not as salty as the vinaigrette). Set aside.

Making the Gnocchi:

step 1 As soon as the potatoes come out of the oven, remove the foil and then peel them.

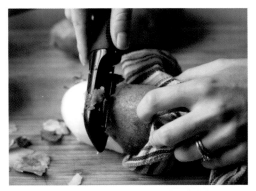

The photo shows me using a vegetable peeler, but I quickly switched to scraping the skin off with the back of a knife—much easier!

step 2 You want to rice the potatoes as soon as they come out of the oven. The hotter the potato, the more steam comes off when you rice it, which reduces the moisture content of the gnocchi. The drier the gnocchi, the less

flour you'll need, which leads to the lightest, fluffiest, most delicious gnocchi. Use a kitchen towel to hold the potato, unless you feel like burning your fingers!

step 3 Now let the potatoes cool/dry for 10 to 15 minutes. During this time, double check that you have everything in place you'll need for shaping, cooking, dressing, and plating the gnocchi. Once they're shaped, you want to be able to cook them and serve them as quickly as possible (unless you'll be freezing the cooked gnocchi for later).

step 4 Gather your cooled potatoes into a flat disc and sprinkle about half of the flour over them.

step 5 Work the dough with your hands, adding more flour if needed. You probably won't need the whole cup of flour. I had about three tablespoons left over. If in doubt, use less as opposed to more.

step 6 Work your dough until just combined. Do not overwork it! It should be soft, not sticky or crumbly. You're not even going to really knead it; just mix it together. You must shape the dough immediately.

step 7 My favorite part! Roll some of the dough out into a long snake, about as

Pasta

thick as your thumb. Cut the snake into little "pillows" and dust them with flour. To shape, simply roll one of the pillows down a ridged gnocchi board (or the tines of a fork). The gnocchi should curl around your thumb. One side will be ridged, and the other side will have an indent in it. This helps to catch the sauce.

step 8 Place the shaped gnocchi on a plate that has been dusted with flour. At this point you should cook the gnocchi immediately. I tried freezing the raw, shaped gnocchi once and it was a disaster! You must at least partially cook the gnocchi at this point or all your hard work will be ruined.

Cooking and Serving the Gnocchi:

step 1 Gently place the gnocchi into the salted, boiling water. After a minute or two, the gnocchi will float to the surface. About 30 seconds after they begin floating, use a slotted spoon to remove them from the water, draining them well.

step 2 Place the cooked gnocchi into a large bowl that has half of the vinaigrette in the bottom. Toss the gnocchi to coat. Drizzle your dinner plates with the other half of the vinaigrette and some of the cream sauce. Pile the gnocchi on the plates and drizzle more cream sauce on top. Garnish with a fresh sprig of thyme and serve immediately.

Hurry Up Alfredo

One day I came home from running errands and I was starving. I felt like pasta with a creamy sauce, but I didn't have the patience to make a roux. I decided to make a blender Alfredo because I didn't care how it turned out and it'd be quick. I not only loved the sauce, but my husband and I now make it on a regular basis. It's fast and easy, and you probably already have all of the ingredients. It's a great compromise between "I don't feel like cooking" and "I don't want to eat toast for dinner." We like it so much, however, that we make it even when we have plenty of time to spend in the kitchen.

I like to use the wide fettucini-style rice noodles, but whatever pasta shape you have will work wonderfully (the shape pictured here is orecchiette). You don't even need pasta to enjoy the sauce: I've made this several times and poured it over a huge bowl of steamed organic broccoli and it was divine.

3 cups of any small pasta shape

Alfredo Sauce

1 cup soy milk

1/3 cup rounded raw, unsalted cashews

1/4 cup nutritional yeast

3 tablespoons low-sodium tamari or soy sauce

2 tablespoons Earth Balance margarine

1 tablespoon tahini

1 tablespoon fresh lemon juice

2 teaspoons Dijon or stone-ground mustard

1/2 teaspoon paprika

1 pinch nutmeg

1 pinch salt

Black pepper, to taste

2 to 4 garlic cloves *(optional)*

Suggested/optional add-ins

2 cups steamed broccoli florets or any other veggie

2 tablespoons of fresh herbs *(your favorite)*

Hurry Up Alfredo

Makes 2 or 3 servings

step 1 Bring a pot of salted water to boil and add the noodles. Cook until tender but not mushy.

step 2 Meanwhile, to make the sauce, mix together the soy milk, cashews, yeast, tamari (or soy sauce), margarine, tahini, lemon juice, mustard, paprika, nutmeg, salt, pepper, and garlic (if using) in a blender and blend on high until very smooth. If your blender is having issues with grinding the nuts smoothly, you can strain the sauce. (Or you can keep them as is and pretend it's a "textural feature.")

step 3 When the noodles are finished cooking, drain them well. Add the noodles back to the now empty but still hot pot and pour as much sauce as you want over them. Turn the heat on and gently stir until the noodles are piping hot, adding in your optional veggies or herbs if you're using them. Serve immediately.

Lime Peanut Noodles with Seitan, Kale, and Carrots

This is a tangy lime noodle dish with a light peanut sauce. The recipe makes what will seem like a very strong sauce, but it will cover enough noodles for four servings, so it needs to be strong. The lime flavor is fairly pronounced, and it's great served warm or as a cold noodle salad. That's a bonus because even if you're not going to have four people eating this, you can make the whole batch and take leftovers to work!

1 package wide, flat rice noodles *(10 ounces)*

¼ cup low-sodium soy sauce or tamari

3 tablespoons peanut butter

2½ tablespoons lime juice, fresh

1 tablespoon sugar

½ teaspoon chili flakes

¼ teaspoon ginger powder *(optional)*

1 to 2 teaspoons of peanut or canola oil

2 cups kale, shredded

1½ cups seitan, cut into strips

1 large carrot, shredded

2 handfuls cashews, crushed *(or substitute peanuts; save some for garnish)*

Lime slice, for garnish

Lime Peanut Noodles with Seitan, Kale, and Carrots

Makes 4 servings

step 1 Begin by boiling water for your rice noodles. While waiting, make the peanut sauce by whisking together the soy sauce, peanut butter, lime juice, sugar, chili flakes, and ginger powder until combined. Set aside.

step 2 Cook the noodles until just softened, then drain and rinse with cold water. Drain well. Use kitchen shears to cut the noodles down to shorter lengths (run your scissors through the noodles until "chopped" or actually chop the noodles with a knife. Uniformly sized noodles makes mixing everything together much easier). Set noodles aside.

step 3 To prepare the kale, seitan, and carrot, heat the oil in a wok over high heat. Add the kale and stir until cooked through and browning in some parts. Add the seitan and carrots, and then turn down the heat a bit.

step 4 Add the noodles to the pan. Add the sauce, reserving about a teaspoon (eyeball it). Stir until everything is well combined, but no longer. If your wok is still super hot, some noodles may stick to the pan, but don't worry.

step 5 Add the nuts to the remaining 1 teaspoon of sauce and toss to coat. Garnish with nuts and a slice of lime and serve immediately or refrigerate for later.

Nearly Raw Tahini Noodles

I use tahini in this recipe, which is a paste made from hulled sesame seeds that is commonly used in the Middle East. The seeds can be raw or roasted, and the flavor will vary depending on which one you choose. My favorite tahini is Arrowhead Mills Organic Sesame Tahini, which is unroasted. It's not too bitter, and it stays smooth and easy to use even after refrigeration. Roasted tahini will also work great in this recipe, but the flavor will be noticeably different.

Sesame paste, on the other hand, is an Asian ingredient that turns the whole sesame seed, including the hulls, into a paste. It's stronger than tahini, so you usually need much less in your recipes, and using too much can cause the dish to be more bitter than you expected. While you can find tahini at any supermarket (look near the peanut butter), Asian sesame paste still seems relegated to specialty markets.

This dish is largely raw, which cuts down on a lot of the work and prevents your summer kitchen from becoming a sauna. I've found that if you cut your veggies small enough and have a great sauce, you'll be surprised at what you can serve raw. If you like, you can lightly steam the broccoli, but it really is tasty simply cut into tiny florets. If you follow a raw food diet, feel free to substitute the cooked wheat noodles with cucumber or zucchini noodles, or whatever raw noodles make you the happiest. Pretty much anything will work as the base of this dish. The other benefit of this dish is that it keeps really well, so I like to make a big batch for lunches, snacks, or meals to go.

Note: This will easily keep for a couple of days. If you're a big fan of sauce, you may want to double the recipe. This recipe makes just enough to coat the noodles. Extra sauce will really come in handy after the completed dish has been refrigerated for a bit; I find noodles really soak up sauces, so it can be nice to have some extra on hand.

If you've tried tahini and disliked it, give it another chance. It's kind of vile on its own, so balancing flavors is very important with this ingredient. If you want a little tahini flavor but can't quite use the full ¼ cup, consider adding some peanut butter in lieu of the tahini. Personally, I find this a really refreshing change from the typical peanut sauces, and since it's so easy to make, why not give it a shot?

Nearly Raw Tahini Noodles

Makes 4 to 6 servings

step 1 Cook the pasta and rinse under cold water. Drain and set aside, coating lightly with oil if desired to prevent the noodles from sticking. These can be made well in advance.

step 2 Cut the cabbage into quarters, using a large chef's knife to remove the core from one of the quarters. Discard the core and wrap up the other three quarters for later use. If you have a food processor, use it to shred the cabbage and carrots. Use the shredder blade that has many holes for the carrots, and the blade that has one single slit for the cabbage. A box grater will work just fine for the carrots and a knife for the cabbage if a food processor is not available.

step 3 Chop the broccoli into small florets, creating pieces no bigger than small grapes.

step 4 Toss all the veggies together and add the pasta.

step 5 To make the tahini sauce, mix together the tahini, tamari, water, agave nectar, vinegar, chili sauce, mustard, salt, and black pepper, tasting to adjust if needed.

step 6 When you're ready to serve, add the sauce to the noodles and veggies and toss with your hands, coating everything evenly. Add chopped mint at the last moment, if using. Garnish with more mint and sesame seeds and serve.

Pasta

½ pound uncooked whole wheat spaghetti

¼ of a green cabbage head, shredded

2 carrots, peeled and shredded

1 stalk broccoli, florets only, cut very small

1 handful fresh mint, chopped *(optional)* or use cilantro or basil instead

Sesame seeds, for garnish

Mint, for garnish

Tahini Sauce:

¼ cup tahini

2 tablespoons low-sodium tamari, Nama Shoyu, or regular soy sauce

3 tablespoons water

1 tablespoon sugar or raw agave nectar

1 tablespoon rice vinegar

1 teaspoon chili sauce or 1 chopped fresh chili

1 teaspoon Dijon or stone-ground mustard

1 pinch salt, if needed

Fresh black pepper, to taste

was so enamored with pad Thai that I never considered ordering anything else when I went out for Thai food. Pad see ew is salty and slightly sweet, unlike its sweet and tangy cousin pad Thai. This is a quick-cooking dish, as it should be, since it's common "street food" in Thailand. You really want to keep the Chinese broccoli crisp, the fresh noodles cook almost instantly, and the gluten just needs to be warmed and coated with sauce. I went from pulling ingredients out of the fridge to eating in 25 minutes. Unfortunately, this dish requires some "specialty" ingredients, but I think (read: hope) the substitutions will be okay.

Pad See Ew

Makes 4 servings

Specialty Ingredients Needed (and Suggested Substitutions):

Chinese broccoli: This is a leafy cross between broccoli and cabbage, and it's awesome. Its stalks look like thick asparagus (or thin broccoli), and its leaves are dark and large. I found bags of it at my Asian grocer, but if you can't find it, I suggest using rapini, broccolini, regular broccoli plus kale and collards, bok choy, or chard.

Chow fun: Chow fun are wide, flat sheet rice noodles that you cut to size yourself. Mine came in long rolls, so it was easy to remove some from the package, slice them, and toss them in. I've read that dry rice noodles become mushy too easily in this dish; fresh chow fun are strongly recommended. If you're going to try dry noodles, I suggest finding the widest rice noodle you can. Slightly undercook it and then shock it in cold water to stop the cooking. Drain very well, as you don't want to add water to the recipe.

Dark soy sauce: It may seem weird to call for two different types of soy sauce in the same recipe, but it really does make a nice flavor for the dish. If you can't find dark soy sauce (that's literally what it's called), use tamari or your regular soy sauce. A combination of Nama Shoyu (for the light) and tamari (for the dark) would work just fine.

3/4 package chow fun *(about 1.8 lbs; see "Specialty Ingredients" page 203)*

2 tablespoons vegetable oil

2 cloves garlic, minced

1/4 teaspoon red pepper flakes *(optional; for very spicy Pad See Ew, use 1/2 teaspoon)*

1 teaspoon grated fresh ginger *(optional)*

1 pound Chinese broccoli, roughly chopped *(pieces should be 1 to 2 inches in length; halve the stems lengthwise to shorten their cooking time)*

1 1/2 cups wheat gluten *(seitan), sliced thin*

3 tablespoons light soy sauce

3 tablespoons dark soy sauce *(or substitute light soy sauce)*

2 tablespoons sugar

step 1 Cut the noodles into 3/4-inch thick pieces (I used about 8 noodle rolls). If curled, unroll them a bit. Don't worry if they break. Here is a shot of what my noodles looked like after I cut them:

step 2 Heat the oil in a large pan or wok. Depending on the size of your cookware, you might need to make two separate batches to serve four, but it cooks quickly so don't worry too much about it. Add the garlic and sauté over medium-low heat until just starting to brown.

step 3 Add pepper flakes and ginger (if using) and cook for 1 minute more.

step 4 Add broccoli and stir-fry until tender crisp, just a few minutes.

step 5 Add gluten, soy sauce, sugar, and cooked noodles. Stir well, cooking for a minute or two. Toss so that the sauce has coated everything well, though it will be light. It's okay if your noodles break up a bit! Cook a few minutes more until the greens are wilted and the stems are no longer raw, but they should still be very crispy. If you cook it too long, your noodles will start to get mushy. Serve immediately with more sugar, soy sauce, and/or chili sauce available at the table. People generally season their Pad see ew outside of the wok to their own tastes.

Vegan Yum Yum

Pasta Gremolata with Sun-dried Tomatoes and Garlic Bread Crumbs

You don't want to make this for a first date. Between the parsley flecks and the garlic, this dish is bound to embarrass you. It's totally worth it though. It's perfect for a simple summer meal, and it also makes a great light lunch. This is your go-to recipe for using up that huge bunch of parsley you bought and can't seem to get through. Gremolata is an Italian salsa verde made with garlic, parsley, and lemon zest. It's traditionally served with osso buco, but it's delicious over pasta. It's pesto without being pesto.

If you don't want to use sun-dried tomatoes, asparagus tips or steamed broccoli florets would work wonderfully instead.

3 cups uncooked rotini

2 tablespoons olive oil

1 to 2 garlic cloves, minced

1/2 cup bread crumbs

Pinch of salt

1/2 cup oil-packed sun-dried tomatoes, cut into strips

1/4 to 1/2 teaspoon red pepper flakes

2 cups fresh flat-leaf parsley, medium packed

Zest from 1 lemon

1 tablespoon olive oil

1 tablespoon pasta water

1/4 teaspoon salt *(kosher or sea salt if you have it)*

Black pepper, to taste

Pasta Gremolata with Sun-dried Tomatoes and Garlic Bread Crumbs

Makes 2 to 3 servings

step 1   Start the water for the pasta, which will cook while you make the other parts of the dish.

step 2   Heat 2 tablespoons of olive oil in a large saucepan (one that will fit your cooked pasta). Add the garlic and sauté until it becomes fragrant, about 30 seconds.

step 3   Add the bread crumbs. They should soak up all the oil, but look shiny. Add a pinch of salt and stir well. Let this sit over low/medium-low heat for about 5 minutes, until the bread crumbs become crispy. If you're worried about them burning, your heat is too high. If you can't hear a little sizzling, your heat is too low. Remove to a small bowl and set aside.

step 4   Place the sun-dried tomatoes in the pan, along with the red pepper flakes. Stir well, keeping them at the same temperature as the bread crumbs. Let these hang out in the pan until the pasta is done. The red pepper flakes will flavor the oil that's left in the pan.

step 5   To make the gremolata, place the parsley in a food processor or blender and pulse until you can't see any more whole leaves, but there are still big chunks. Grate the lemon zest on top of the parsley, pulse twice more to combine, then scoop everything out into a large bowl. (You may also chop the parsley by hand.)

step 6   Add the olive oil, pasta water, and salt to the parsley/lemon zest mixture. Mix.

step 7   When the pasta is cooked al dente (firm, but still cooked), drain well (you don't want to add too much water) and place it in the large pan with the tomatoes and red pepper flakes. Toss.

step 8   Pour the pasta and tomatoes into the bowl containing the gremolata. Toss again, being sure to evenly distribute the sauce over the pasta. Taste, adding salt or a squirt of lemon juice if needed. Grind fresh pepper over the top. Top with the garlic bread crumbs. Serve immediately.

Pepita Fettucini with Spinach and Cranberries

In an effort to get excited about autumn, I've been doing my best to pick up some new ingredients. Goodness knows I never look forward to winter, so food may be the only way I can actually celebrate the changing of the seasons. One of the ingredients I picked up one season was a tub of organic pepitas. Pepitas are pumpkin seeds that are usually sold with the white hull removed, revealing a smooth olive green seed. If you decide to use pumpkin seeds from the pumpkins you carve this year, be sure to wash and dry the seeds thoroughly and roast them in a low oven for an hour or so until dry and toasty. Don't worry about removing the white hull.

This pasta is flavored with a dab of tamari and maple syrup, which coats the pasta and gives it a nice, balanced, sweet flavor. The spinach is sautéed with red pepper flakes for a bit of heat, the cranberries add a pop of sweet tanginess, and the crushed pepitas round out the whole dish. It's really a lovely meal, and what's more, it's super easy to prepare: it should only take as long to make this dish as the pasta takes to cook. I made it for lunch, so this recipe only serves one, but it's very easy to increase the servings should you want to make it for more than one person.

Pepita Fettucini with Spinach and Cranberries

Makes 1 serving

step 1 Bring a pot of salted water to boil and add the fettucini. While the pasta is cooking, pulse the pepitas in your food processor or blender until chopped fairly fine, then set aside.

step 2 Heat the oil in a large skillet over medium heat and add the spinach. Use tongs to coat the spinach in the hot oil. Add the red pepper flakes, tamari, and maple syrup, and then the thyme if you're using it. Toss in the cranberries and mix everything well. Turn the heat to low (or just turn it off and cover it until your pasta is cooked).

step 3 Once the pasta is done, drain it and add it to the skillet. Add the chopped pepitas and toss well until everything is coated. Taste a noodle and see if you need an extra splash of tamari and/or maple syrup. The noodles should look like they don't have sauce on them, but they'll taste like they do. Serve immediately.

Ingredients

Fettucini for one

$1/3$ cup raw, unsalted pepitas or pumpkin seeds

1 tablespoon oil

2 large handfuls spinach, torn

$1/4$ teaspoon red pepper flakes

1 tablespoon tamari or soy sauce

1 tablespoon maple syrup

2 to 3 fresh thyme sprigs *(optional)*

$1/4$ cup dried cranberries

Rigatoni with Fresh Grape Tomato Sauce

This is one of my all-time favorite tomato sauces. Grape tomatoes are super sweet, making for a really refreshing sauce, and they cook down in about 10 minutes. You can easily put this sauce together in the time it takes for your noodles to boil.

Vegan Yum Yum

Rigatoni with Fresh Grape Tomato Sauce

Makes 2 servings

step 1   Heat a large pot of boiling, salted water and cook pasta until al dente.

step 2   Meanwhile, heat the oil in a sauté pan. Add the garlic and herbs and sauté until the garlic begins to soften. Add the tomatoes and toss well. The tomatoes will burst on their own when they get hot enough, but you may want to pierce them with a knife or squish them to break the skins.

step 3   Add salt and cook for 10 to 15 minutes, until tomatoes are fully cooked and the sauce is rich and thick. Season with black pepper to taste. Add optional ingredients, if desired. Add cooked rigatoni to the pan and toss to coat. Serve.

Ingredients

3 cups dried rigatoni

3 tablespoons olive oil

2 cloves garlic, sliced, optional

$1\frac{1}{2}$ teaspoons dried Italian herbs

2 pints sweet grape tomatoes

$\frac{3}{4}$ to 1 teaspoon salt

Black pepper, to taste

Optional add-ins:

1 small handful fresh basil

$\frac{1}{2}$ teaspoon balsamic vinegar

$\frac{1}{2}$ teaspoon red pepper flakes for heat

1 cup baby spinach or other greens

Roasted Cauliflower and Wilted Spinach Salad

W e love pasta salads in the summer, but the ingredients in this pasta salad make it perfect any time of the year. This travels well, so bring it along to potlucks, picnics, or pack it up for lunch at work. You can use kalamata olives, too, instead of the sun-dried tomatoes.

Roasted Cauliflower and Wilted Spinach Salad

Makes 4 servings

step 1 Preheat the oven to 400°F and put a pot of salted water on to boil.

step 2 Place the cauliflower in a baking pan in one layer. Add the olive oil, dried herbs, salt, and pepper and toss with the cauliflower. Roast for 20 to 30 minutes until just beginning to brown and fork-tender, but *not* mushy. Turn the oven to broil and broil for 1 to 3 minutes until nicely colored.

step 3 Cook the pasta, then drain and rinse in cool water. Toss with a small amount of olive oil to prevent sticking, if not using immediately.

step 4 Place the spinach in a large bowl. Dump the hot cauliflower on top of the spinach and gently toss. Set aside and let the heat from the cauliflower wilt the spinach. Add the pasta on top.

step 5 Add the tomatoes and vinegar and toss well. Add more olive oil if needed. Season to taste with more salt/pepper and vinegar—until the flavors really pop—and then serve.

Ingredients

1 head cauliflower, chopped into bite-size pieces

1/4 cup olive oil

1/2 tablespoon dried herbs of your choice *(basil, marjoram, oregano, and thyme work well)*

1/2 teaspoon kosher salt

Black pepper, to taste

3 cups penne pasta

4 cups baby spinach

1/2 cup oil-packed sun-dried tomatoes, cut into strips

1 tablespoon balsamic vinegar *(more if needed)*

Seven Spice Udon

I invented this dish one night when I was looking for a midnight snack. It's best with the dry udon noodles that come in packs of five-noodle bundles. Pan-frying them in a nonstick skillet or a well-seasoned cast-iron skillet gives the noodles a nice crunchy texture here and there, but the real secret is the spice mix. Use Shichimi Togarashi (aka Japanese Seven Spice) generously on these noodles. The mixture varies depending on the brand, but mine contains orange peel, black, white, and toasted sesame seeds, cayenne pepper, ginger, poppy seeds, Szechuan pepper, and nori (seaweed). You can mix your own if you can find all the ingredients (the orange peel is key!), but it'll be far easier and far less expensive to purchase a bottle at a local Asian grocer or online.

Vegan Yum Yum

Seven Spice Udon

Makes 2 servings

step 1   Cook udon noodles in boiling, salted water for 4 minutes, or for as long as the package directs. Rinse with cool water and coat very lightly with oil to prevent sticking.

step 2   Heat 2 teaspoons of the oil in a nonstick sauté pan and cook the shredded Brussels sprouts and carrots with 1/4 teaspoon Seven Spice until just tender, about 2 minutes. Set aside.

step 3   In the same nonstick pan, heat 1 to 2 tablespoons of oil. Add the noodles and let them cook over high heat for several minutes without disturbing them. The noodles should turn golden brown on the bottom and begin to form a noodle pancake. Turn the noodles and add the cooked vegetables, along with the soy sauce, rice vinegar, and remaining Seven Spice. Once heated through, with some of the noodles crispy and golden and others soft, serve.

Ingredients

3 small bunches dried udon noodles

2 to 3 tablespoons oil, for cooking

5 Brussels sprouts, shredded

1 large carrot, shredded

1 3/4 teaspoons Japanese Seven Spice, split into 1/4 and 1 1/2 teaspoon amounts

3 tablespoons soy sauce

2 tablespoons rice vinegar

Super Quick Tomato Basil Cream Pasta

During the summertime, I can't get enough of recipes that use fresh tomatoes and basil. But no matter what time of year, I'm always down with quick recipes. You can make this sauce in the time it takes to boil the pasta, so this simple sauce makes a 9-minute meal that's hard to beat. Cashews are the base of most of my favorite vegan cream sauces because they're very rich tasting and blend easily, allowing you to create a velvety smooth sauce in your blender.

Vegan Yum Yum

Super Quick Tomato Basil Cream Pasta

Makes 2 servings

step 1 Bring a large pot of salted water to a boil and cook the pasta according to the directions on the package.

step 2 As the pasta is cooking, core the tomato, then roughly chop it. Add it to your blender, seeds, skin, and all. Add the cashews, water, and tomato paste. Blend until very smooth.

step 3 Add the olive oil to a large sauté pan over medium-high heat. Add the garlic and sauté until golden, being careful not to burn it.

step 4 Pour the sauce from the blender into the sauté pan and bring to a simmer. Add the salt and let it cook for 4 to 5 minutes, stirring occasionally.

step 5 If desired, add the wine or water to thin out the sauce. Taste and season, if necessary. Let it simmer until the pasta is finished cooking.

step 6 Once the pasta is cooked, drain it well. Add the pasta to the sauté pan with the black pepper and freshly chopped basil leaves. Toss it to coat. Serve immediately, garnishing with more pepper and basil.

Ingredients

6 to 8 ounces uncooked whole-wheat spaghetti

1 to 2 large, ripe tomatoes

$1/2$ cup raw cashews

$1/4$ cup water

1 tablespoon tomato paste

2 tablespoons olive oil

2 to 4 cloves garlic, minced *(optional)*

1 teaspoon salt

2 to 3 tablespoons wine or water *(optional)*

1 to 2 teaspoons freshly cracked, coarse black pepper

1 large handful fresh basil leaves, chopped

chapter eight

Desserts

Apple Strudel

This dessert is super easy to throw together, even at the last minute. Surprisingly, the most common brand of puff pastry sold at the grocery stores is actually vegan. It's not the healthiest puff pastry in the world, but it's definitely vegan, easy to use, and easy to find. Check the freezer section for it; it's sold in sheets that come in a narrow, rectangular box. Keep one in your freezer and you'll always be prepared.

Apple Strudel

Makes 6 servings

step 1 Defrost the puff pastry according to package directions (it takes approximately 30 to 40 minutes to defrost one sheet).

step 2 Preheat the oven to 375°F.

step 3 Combine the sugar, flour, cinnamon, nutmeg, allspice, and salt. Toss the sliced apples with the lemon juice and then coat with the dry spice mixture.

step 4 Unfold the puff pastry and roll out to 11 x 14 inches.

Ingredients

1 puff pastry sheet, defrosted

3 tablespoons sugar

1½ tablespoons all-purpose flour

½ teaspoon cinnamon

1 pinch nutmeg

1 pinch allspice

1 pinch salt

2 to 3 apples, peeled and sliced thinly

1 tablespoon lemon juice

2 tablespoons Earth Balance margarine, melted

Sugar, for sanding

step 5 Place the apples in a line down the middle.

step 6 Fold the dough over and tuck in the ends.

step 7 Brush the strudel with melted margarine and sand generously with sugar.

step 8 Using a serrated knife, make several diagonal slashes in the strudel.

step 9 Bake for 35 minutes until golden and puffy. Let it cool for an additional 20 to 30 minutes before slicing, then serve.

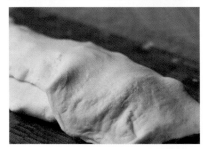

Vegan Yum Yum

Banana Bread Made with Spelt

There are a million banana bread recipes out there, but it's hard to find a decent recipe for spelt banana bread. Spelt is an early form of wheat, so while it still has gluten in it, many people find it easier to digest. I find it tastier than plain ol' wheat and often reach for it to make up part or all of my baked goods. Due to spelt's delicate gluten structure, your bread won't rise as high as wheat, but it'll make up for its smaller stature in taste!

You can substitute regular wheat for this recipe, of course, but you may need to add a touch more liquid to compensate for the change. Add a splash of water or your favorite nondairy milk if you need to. Also, experiment with all-purpose and spelt blends. A ratio of 50:50 gives you the benefits of both flours.

3 very ripe bananas, mashed

1 cup sugar

½ cup vegetable oil

2 teaspoon vanilla extract

2 teaspoons molasses

2 cups spelt flour *(or all-purpose flour)*

½ cup all-purpose flour

½ teaspoon salt

1 teaspoon cinnamon

2 pinches nutmeg

1 teaspoon baking powder

Banana Bread made with Spelt

Makes 1 loaf

step 1   Preheat the oven to 350°F.

step 2   Mash the bananas very well in a bowl. Add sugar, oil, vanilla, and molasses.

step 3   In another bowl, mix together the flour (both kinds), salt, cinnamon, nutmeg, and baking powder. Gently fold the dry ingredients into the wet. If you used all-purpose flour, you may need to add a splash of liquid.

step 4   Bake in a greased 9-x-5 loaf pan for 60 to 70 minutes. Let cool before removing from the pan.

Blueberry Grunts

Yeah, I'd never heard of a blueberry grunt, either—until I became friends with Sandy. Ever since we became friends, I couldn't use the word "blueberry" without her saying "Mmmm, blueberry grunt . . ." with her eyes half closed and smiling. I knew it was one of her favorite desserts, but I couldn't bring myself to make something called a grunt—until, that is, I had four cups of freshly picked blueberries.

A grunt is in the cobbler family, and it's a traditional East Coast maritime dessert. It's perfect for people who might want something like a pie but are too lazy to make an actual pie. So that means it's perfect for me! Blueberry is a popular flavor for grunts, but you can use pretty much any berry or fruit. It's a great way to use up bountiful—but fleeting—summer fruit.

The most common way to make a grunt is to boil berries with water, sugar, and lemon juice, then add biscuit dough on the top, cover with a tight lid, and steam. It's a one-pan, stove-top operation. I chose to bake mine because I had these ridiculously cute gratin dishes that I'd been dying to use for a blog post, but I've also given directions for cooking it on the stove. Recipes for grunts are all pretty standard; I adapted and veganized this simple recipe.

Blueberry Filling

4 cups fresh blueberries *(or frozen)*

³/₄ cup sugar

1 tablespoon lemon juice

¹/₂ cup water

¹/₂ teaspoon cinnamon *(optional)*

¹/₂ teaspoon nutmeg *(optional)*

Simple Biscuits

2 cups all-purpose flour

4 teaspoons baking powder

¹/₂ teaspoon salt

3 tablespoons Earth Balance margarine or vegetable shortening

³/₄ to 1 cup soy milk

Blueberry Grunts

Makes 4 individual grunts or 1 large

step 1 Put the blueberries, sugar, lemon juice, water, and cinnamon and nutmeg (if using) into a large skillet (with a tight-fitting lid if you're going to be making one large grunt and steaming the biscuits; if you're going to be baking the grunt, make sure you're using an oven-safe skillet). If you're baking the grunt, preheat the oven to 400°F.

step 2 Boil the berries for 10 to 15 minutes until the mixture has thickened a little.

step 3 Meanwhile, to make the biscuits, combine the flour, baking powder, and salt. Using a pastry cutter or a fork, cut the margarine (or shortening) into the dry ingredients until it resembles a crumbly mixture. If your berries aren't done yet, put the dry mixture into the fridge or freezer to keep the margarine cold until you're ready to finish it.

step 4 When the berries are done cooking, add the soy milk to the dry mixture to form a soft biscuit dough. The consistency is pretty forgiving—a slightly too-soft or too-firm dough won't make a difference in the final product. As long as it holds together, but is soft enough

Vegan Yum Yum

to break apart into clumps, you're good to go. Don't overmix the dough, or the biscuits will be tough (but you already knew that, right?).

Stove-top directions if you're making one large steamed grunt:

Break the biscuit dough up into small, bite-size pieces. Spread the pieces evenly on top of the hot, still-cooking berries. Cover the skillet with a tight-fitting lid, reduce the heat slightly, and steam for 15 minutes without peeking. The biscuits should be puffed up and cooked all the way through. Serve warm.

Baking directions for one large baked grunt:

Follow the instructions for a steamed grunt, but place in the oven to bake at 400°F (without a lid) for 20 minutes. You can sand the biscuits with sugar before baking if you like! Serve warm.

For individual baked grunts:

Put the berry mixture into individual ramekins or gratin dishes, filling only until they're half full. Add biscuit mixture on top. Sand with sugar and place all the grunts on a baking sheet (this will help you take them out of the oven without burning yourself). Bake for 20 minutes, serve warm.

Here's what my individual grunts looked like before baking:

Serving suggestions: These are great just as they are, but you can also serve them with some ice cream if you want. I invited Sandy over to try them, and she said that not only were they delicious, but they tasted "exactly like a nonvegan grunt." So if you're looking for a simple but elegant dessert to use up summer berries, I highly recommend this one. I won't blame you if you call it a cobbler, though.

Cherry Trifles

You can use a standard-size trifle dish for this recipe, but what's the fun in that? I first made this recipe using individual-size trifle dishes, but they just weren't quite small enough, and I ended up being overwhelmed by this very beautiful but sweet dessert. Then it hit me: drinking glasses! Do you have shot glasses in your cupboard? They make the cutest, most adorable super-mini trifles, perfect for a tiny treat at the end of your meal. But don't limit yourself to shot glasses—almost any glass will do.

Before assembling the trifles, the almond pudding, cherry filling, and the sponge cake need to be prepared and cooled. I find it easiest to make the almond pudding and cherry filling the night before, and then I bake the cake on the day I'm planning on serving the trifles. This ensures that the cake is fresh and moist. Fully assembled trifles can also be made ahead of time and refrigerated before serving; they taste extra good this way.

Vegan Yum Yum

Cherry Trifles

Makes 4 miniature trifles or 1 large trifle

step 1 To make the almond pudding, whisk together the soy milk, rice syrup, powdered sugar, vanilla extract, and almond extract in a large pot. Place the cornstarch in a bowl. Pour a little bit of your liquid pudding mixture into your cornstarch mixture ($1/4$ cup or so). Whisk the cornstarch/pudding mixture until smooth and add it back into the pot. Whisk well. Cook the pudding over medium heat, whisking constantly, until thickened. It won't be super thick, but it should coat the back of a spoon well. (Note: You may need to turn your heat up to get your pudding to thicken. This should be your first problem-solving step if your pudding is not changing consistency. If you have turned your heat up higher and the pudding is very hot but still not thickening, you may need to add more cornstarch. Never add dry cornstarch to a hot mixture or you will get lumps. Instead, mix the cornstarch with a little cold or warm liquid and then stir it into the pudding mixture.) This can take up to 10 minutes.

step 2 Once the pudding seems to be fully thickened, put it into a bowl and chill until cold.

step 3 To make the cherry filling, it is easiest to use frozen cherries. Simply add the cherries, sugar, lemon juice, lemon zest, and cornstarch mixture to a pot over medium heat and stir well until the cherries are defrosted and the filling has thickened. Remove from the heat and let chill. You may want to have some fresh cherries on hand for garnishing.

Desserts

Almond Pudding

4 cups soy milk

$2/3$ cup brown rice syrup

$1/4$ cup powdered sugar

2 teaspoons vanilla extract

2 teaspoons almond extract

$1/2$ cup cornstarch

Cherry Filling

3 bags of frozen dark sweet cherries *(or 6 to 7 cups fresh dark cherries, pitted)*

2 cups sugar

$1/2$ cup lemon juice

Zest of 2 lemons

3 tablespoons cornstarch plus 3 tablespoons water, mixed

Ingredients

(Ingredients continued on next page)

Sponge Cake

Ingredients

1⅓ cups soy milk mixed with 1 teaspoon apple cider vinegar

2 cups all-purpose flour

1 cup sugar

2 teaspoons baking powder

1 teaspoon baking soda

1 tablespoon cornstarch

½ teaspoon salt

¼ cup vegetable oil

1 teaspoon vanilla extract

1 teaspoon almond extract

Chocolate shavings (optional)

Sprinkles (optional)

If you're using fresh cherries: Wash and set aside 20 of the prettiest cherries that have stems intact. Wash and pit the remainder and add them to a large pot. Add the sugar, lemon juice, lemon zest, and cornstarch mixture and turn heat up to medium-high. Mush some of the cherries with your spoon, but leave the majority whole. Cook until the cherries are softened and the filling has thickened up a bit.

step 4 To make the cake, preheat the oven to 375°F and grease two 8 x 8-inch baking pans. Add the apple cider vinegar to the soy milk and set aside.

step 5 Whisk the flour, sugar, baking powder, baking soda, cornstarch, and salt together in a large bowl.

step 6 Add the oil and vanilla and almond extracts to the soy milk mixture and mix, then add the liquid mixture to the dry ingredients and mix until there are no lumps or just a few small lumps.

step 7 Spread the batter out evenly between the two baking pans. Bake for 18 to 22 minutes or until golden on the top, a toothpick tests clean, and the cake springs back to your touch. Let cool.

step 8 Once the cakes are cool, place the trifle dish on top on the cake and use a sharp knife to trace around the dish, just breaking the "skin" of the cake. Press the trifle dish down into the cake, twisting as you do so. If needed, use the knife again to cut all the way through. Remove the round piece of cake. Repeat until you have gotten as many rounds out of each cake as you can, depending on what size dish you've used. Each round should be 1 inch tall.

step 9 Using a sharp knife, carefully slice each round in half horizontally, making two ½-inch-thick rounds. Cover with plastic wrap until ready for assembling.

step 10 To assemble the trifles, place a dollop of cherry filling into the trifle dish, then add a cake round, pushing it down into the bottom of the dish. Add some pudding on top of that, then cherry filling, and another round. Press down. Add one more layer of pudding. This should bring you to the top of the glass. Top with optional chocolate shavings or sprinkles. Add fresh cherries as a garnish and serve or refrigerate until serving. (Note that larger trifles will use more than two rounds of cake—you should have four to work with.)

Honeydew Coconut Tapioca

This dessert has a lot of bang for its buck. Visually stunning and super delicious, it requires minimal effort to put together. It's quickest to make if you look for the semihydrated tapioca pearls that are sold for boba tea drinks (aka bubble tea), but you can make it with traditional tapioca as well.

Honeydew Coconut Tapioca

Makes 4 to 6 servings

step 1   Cook the tapioca according to package directions.

step 2   Heat the coconut milk over medium heat and stir in the sugar until dissolved.

step 3   Using a melon baller, make several melon balls from the honeydew.

step 4   Scoop the tapioca pearls into serving dishes. Top with sweetened coconut milk. Add melon balls to the top and a sprig of mint to garnish if desired. Serve.

1 cup black semidried tapioca pearls

1 14-ounce can coconut milk

3 tablespoons sugar

$1/2$ ripe honeydew melon

Fresh mint for garnish *(optional)*

Miniature Baked Doughnuts

I set out to create a vegan doughnut recipe that didn't involve frying. All you need is a "petite doughnut pan," which should be available at kitchen stores or online. Look for something nonstick. My standard party dessert has been cupcakes up till now, but now that I know how easy doughnuts are to make, I've been converted.

Miniature Baked Doughnuts

Makes 20 doughnuts

step 1 Preheat the oven to 350°F.

step 2 In a large bowl, combine the flour, sugar, baking powder, salt, nutmeg, and cinnamon with a whisk to mix thoroughly.

step 3 Combine the soy milk, apple cider vinegar, vanilla extract, egg substitute, and margarine in a small saucepan over medium-low heat and mix until the margarine is melted. This mixture should not get too hot; you should be able to stick your finger in the mixture and feel slightly warm. If you burn yourself: (1) it's not my fault! and (2) it's too hot for the dough!

step 4 Add the wet ingredients to the dry ingredients and mix until just combined. It should form a very soft dough or thick batter.

step 5 Using a tablespoon measure, scoop out the dough into the ungreased, nonstick mini-doughnut pan. Smooth out the top of the doughnuts with your fingers, clearing off the post in the middle of each one. This will make for more even, prettier doughnuts, but isn't crucial. If you overfill, your doughnuts will come out looking like they have muffin tops. While not the end of the world, it's not very doughnut-like either.

step 6 Bake for 12 minutes until the doughnuts are almost browned on top and a toothpick comes out clean. Invert the hot pan over a cutting board or cool-

Special Equipment Needed

Petite doughnut pan

1 cup all-purpose flour

$1/2$ cup sugar

$1 1/2$ teaspoons baking powder

$1/4$ teaspoon salt

$1/4$ teaspoon *(scant)* nutmeg

1 tiny pinch *(or shake)* cinnamon

$1/2$ cup soy milk

$1/2$ teaspoon apple cider vinegar

$1/2$ teaspoon pure vanilla extract

Egg substitute for 1 egg

4 tablespoons Earth Balance margarine

Ingredients

ing rack to release the doughnuts. Allow to cool completely before decorating (unless you're making powdered sugar doughnuts; see instructions below). If you let them cool loosely covered with plastic wrap, the donuts will stay soft and fluffy.

Decorating Directions

Chocolate-dipped Doughnuts: This is the easy part. Melt 1 bar of your favorite dark chocolate in the microwave. Remove from the microwave and stir every 15 seconds until chocolate is smooth and barely warm to the touch. I should mention that you should be very careful not to get any water in the chocolate or it could seize up, and no one likes that! Dip your doughnuts one by one into the chocolate, then place on a wire rack and sprinkle with sprinkles.

Glazed Doughnuts with Sprinkles: Whisk together 1/2 cup lump-free powdered sugar with 1 tablespoon of soy milk. Dip the "bottom" half of the doughnut (the side with the nicer shape) into the glaze, let some drip off, then dip glazed side down into a bowlful of sprinkles (1/4 to 1/2 cup). Transfer to a wire rack that has been set on top of some parchment paper (or wax paper). The excess glaze will drip through the rack onto the paper for easy cleanup later.

Powdered Sugar Doughnuts: While the doughnuts are still warm from the oven, roll them in a bowl of powdered sugar.

Striped Doughnuts: Dip doughnuts into the powdered sugar glaze (see glazed doughnuts above for glaze recipe), then drizzle with melted chocolate.

Mini Blueberry Tarts with Lemon Cream

Whoa-my-god. I love tarts! The secret to the lemon cream is coconut milk. Shh! It gives it a rich, fatty feel (like cream), but it's not enough to make it taste too coconutty. Discerning palates will still taste the tofu, but it's really not bad. I wouldn't include it if it was bad, would I? (I've included instructions for 8 mini tarts or 1 large one.)

Special Equipment Needed

Individual mini tart pans with removable bottoms or large tart pan with a removable bottom (can be purchased at most kitchen stores or online)

Tart Dough

1½ cups whole-wheat pastry flour (218 g)

¼ cup sugar

¼ teaspoon salt

¼ cup Earth Balance margarine

¼ cup shortening

3 to 4 tablespoons cold water

Lemon Cream

1 package Mori-Nu Silken Extra Firm Tofu, drained as much as you can

½ cup powdered sugar

½ cup coconut milk

4 teaspoons lemon juice

1 teaspoon vanilla

Zest of 1 lemon

Other Ingredients

Fruit jelly, any flavor

2 pints organic blueberries

Powdered sugar

Mint sprigs

Lemon zest

Mini Blueberry Tarts with Lemon Cream

Makes 8 mini 4-inch tarts or 1 large tart

step 1 To make the dough, mix the whole-wheat pastry flour, sugar, and salt together. Cut the margarine and shortening into the flour mixture with a food processor, in a bowl with a pastry cutter, or with your hands. You want every flour grain coated with the fat. It should look like wet sand with little pea-size lumps in it when it's ready. Do your best not to overwork the dough.

step 2 Add in the water, one tablespoon at a time, until the dough holds together. It's easier to add more water than to add more flour, so be conservative.

step 3 Turn out the dough onto a lightly floured surface and *gently* knead (or really, press) it together. Adjust with more water or flour as needed. Shape into a flat round, cover in plastic wrap, and refrigerate for at least an hour.

step 4 Make the lemon cream by blending the tofu, powdered sugar, coconut milk, lemon juice, vanilla, and lemon zest in a food processor or blender until very smooth. Scrape the mixture into a bowl, cover with plastic wrap, and refrigerate until needed. The cream should be very soft, but not drippy. You should be able to bite into the tart and not have it pour out all over you, even if the tart is at room temperature.

Vegan Yum Yum

step 5 Lightly oil your mini tart pan or one large tart pan, taking care to oil each of the ridges on the sides. I know—it's a pain, but it's more of a pain to break your tart shells because they stick.

Making Mini Tarts:

step 1 Remove the dough from the refrigerator. Roll it out onto a lightly floured surface to ¼-inch (or slightly less) thick. Cut out rough squares or circles a little larger than the tart pan.

step 2 Gently lay the dough over the tart shell and ease it in, paying attention to the sides. Pinch off the overhanging dough.

step 3 Using a finger with a short nail, press the dough into each of the ridges around the shell. Lightly prick the surface and edges with a fork.

step 4 Repeat for all shells. If needed, gather scraps, form into a ball, and roll out again until your shells are made.

Making One Large Tart:

Remove the dough from the refrigerator and roll out onto lightly floured parchment paper or plastic wrap to ¼-inch (or slightly less) thick. Gently lift the dough by the parchment or plastic wrap and overturn it onto your tart pan. Ease the dough into the mold, paying attention to the sides. Pinch off the overhanging dough. Using a finger with a short nail, press the dough into each of the ridges around the inside of the tart pan. Lightly prick the surface and edges with a fork.

Baking instructions (for both sizes):

step 1 Preheat the oven to 375°F.

step 2 Place parchment paper on top of your tart(s). Fill the shells (or shell if using a large tart pan) with dried beans (I used garbanzos because that's all I had), making sure that they fill the molds. Place tart(s) onto a cookie sheet (that way you won't accidentally pop the bottoms up and mess up your dough when you're moving them) and refrigerate for 15 minutes.

step 3 Place the pan(s) directly into the oven and bake for 10 minutes. Then take the pan(s) from the oven, remove the parch-

ment paper and beans (don't burn yourself!), and place back into the oven for another 5 to 7 minutes or until the tart shells are just beginning to turn golden. Be careful not to burn your shells! They will go from golden to burned in the blink of an eye.

step 4 Remove the tart shells from the oven and let them cool on a wire rack until cool enough to handle. Then *gently* remove shells from their molds by lightly pressing up on the bottom of the mold. Then slide the bottom piece off to the side and place the tart shells back onto the rack to cool completely.

step 5 Put a couple of tablespoons of jelly into a bowl and mix with a small amount of water until it looks like a glaze. Brush your tart shells with the glaze. This will give them a shiny, professional appearance, as well as prevent them from drying out as fast. Apricot is traditional, but I used violet jelly. The jelly glaze should be thin enough not to affect the color of the shells, and perhaps that's one of the reasons why apricot is traditional—it's pretty much the same color as the curst.

step 6 Fill your tart shell(s) about halfway with the chilled lemon cream, and then pick over your blueberries—you want only pretty berries for your tart! Begin placing the berries, "ruffled" side up in the shell along the edge in a circle. Try to pick berries that are the same size. Continue to place concentric rings of berries into the shell until you reach the center. Add the last berry.

step 7 Using a brush or your fingers, lightly coat the berries in the jelly glaze as well. Chill until ready to serve. Before serving, lightly dust the tarts with powdered sugar, add a sprig of mint, and plate with fresh lemon zest.

Sheera

Sheera is an Indian dessert or breakfast that is similar to American Cream of Wheat, but it's thicker and a lot more fun. The base is called "sooji" or "semolina" and is easily substituted for quick-cooking Cream of Wheat. I'm not entirely convinced that there's actually a difference between the two.

Sheera can be made into a sweet or savory meal, and both are loved because they're quick to throw together and very comforting. I was told that there is never an excuse not to have dessert when you can have sheera. Here is the recipe for the sweet version, spiced with cardamom and flecked with fried raisins and cashews. Saffron gives it a color and flavor boost, but it's an optional ingredient. When Nanni made this for us, she actually broke out food coloring to tint it a rich yellow! She originally used golden raisins, but I couldn't find any at the store, so I used regular. They are stronger tasting than the golden raisins, but they provide a nice burst of color.

Sheera

Makes 4 dessert servings

step 1 Heat water to boiling. A teakettle works great; just heat 2½ cups or so and keep it hot so you can measure out and add 2 cups of hot water to the sooji when you need it.

step 2 Prepare the cardamom by breaking open all of the pods and separating the seeds from the husk. Using a mortar and pestle or the bottom of a glass (or whatever you want), crush the seeds to a fine powder and set aside.

step 3 Heat 2 tablespoons of the oil over medium-high heat in a medium-size pot. Add the cashews and fry, stirring constantly, until golden brown. Remove from the bowl with a slotted spoon, leaving the oil in the pan.

step 4 Add the raisins and fry until they lighten in color and puff up like weird little alien raisins, about 1 minute. Remove them with a slotted spoon, placing them in the bowl with the cashews.

step 5 Turn the heat down to medium, add the sooji, and stir well, until it absorbs the oil and looks like slightly wet sand. Add the cardamom, cashews, raisins, sugar, and saffron (if using) and mix well. Turn down the heat and add 2 cups of boiling water, stirring well. Add the remaining tablespoon of oil and stir until the mixture gets very thick, about 2 to 3 minutes. Serve immediately.

Ingredients

2 cups boiling water

10 green cardamom pods

3 tablespoons canola oil, divided into 2 and 1

¼ cup raw, unsalted cashews

¼ cup raisins *(golden or regular)*

¾ cup sooji *(or quick-cooking Cream of Wheat)*

½ cup sugar

¼ teaspoon saffron *(optional)*

Snickerdoodles

I love snickerdoodles. Plain sugar cookies just don't do it for me, but roll them in a little cinnamon sugar and I'm sold. (Roll nearly anything in cinnamon sugar and I'm sold.) This is a cookie that performs beautifully when veganized. If you have a family recipe you use, I can almost guarantee you that all you need to do is substitute Earth Balance margarine for the butter and Ener-G Egg Replacer for the eggs and you'll be set. Here is a recipe I made after checking out several different snickerdoodle recipes. It's fast, easy, and pretty near fail-proof.

One thing you should know: The temperature of the cookie dough as it goes into the oven determines the shape and overall look of the cookies. If you want cookies that are pillowy and show a lot of cracks and texture, the dough needs to be fairly cold as it goes into the oven. If you like thinner, more even-looking cookies, let the dough warm up a little before baking. If the dough is cold, the cookies don't have much time to warm up and flatten out before the outside of the cookie bakes and prevents further expansion. If it's already a little warm, the cookies will expand and spread (and flatten) in the first few minutes of cooking. The pictures here are cookies baked when the dough was cold. These cookies are a snap if you make them in a stand mixer but only take slightly more elbow grease if you're doing them by hand. And they ship beautifully.

1 cup sugar

½ cup Earth Balance margarine

1 teaspoon vanilla extract

1½ teaspoons Ener-G Egg Replacer mixed with 2 tablespoons hot water

1½ cups all-purpose flour

¼ teaspoon cream of tartar

¼ teaspoon baking soda

Cinnamon sugar, for rolling

Snickerdoodles

Makes approximately 18 cookies

step 1 Cream the sugar, margarine, and vanilla extract together with a wooden spoon or a fork (or beat together in a stand mixer) in a medium-size bowl.

step 2 In a small bowl, whisk the egg replacer and water until foamy. Add it to the margarine and sugar mixture, then whip (or whisk) it all together until it's light and fluffy.

step 3 In a separate bowl, mix the flour, cream of tartar, and baking soda. Add approximately ⅔ of the dry ingredients to the whipped mixture and then whip until combined. Add in the remaining flour and mix by hand. Cover the dough with plastic wrap and refrigerate for 1 hour.

step 4 Preheat the oven to 375°F.

step 5 When the dough is chilled, line a cookie sheet with parchment paper. Using a small ice-cream scoop or 2 tablespoons, make balls of dough. Roll each ball in cinnamon sugar.

step 6 Using a fork (or whatever you want), lightly flatten the dough balls into discs that are approximately ¼-inch thick.

step 7 Bake for 10 minutes for chewy cookies or 12 minutes for crunchy ones. Remove from the oven and let them sit for 30 seconds. They'll be very soft when they come out of the oven, but that's just fine! Gently remove the cookies from the baking sheet and let them cool for a few minutes on a wire rack before serving.

Vegan Yum Yum

chapter nine

Cheers to Delicious Drinks

Boba Tea Two Ways

Forget the prepackaged boba tea mixes that cost $10 a bag and aren't even vegan. Make your own. This may require a Vita-Mix, but you can try it in a regular blender or a food processor. This recipe depends on freeze-dried fruit. You can find this at Whole Foods (the Just Strawberries brand) or at Trader Joe's. Trader Joe's also offers ranbutan, pineapple, and some other interesting choices. One package of the Trader Joe's strawberries was used here; it equals about 2 cups. Experiment! Have fun! (The strawberry boba tea mix doesn't actually contain tea, like most of the fruit boba flavors. Stay tuned for actual tea variations.)

Vegan Yum Yum

Strawberry Ranbutan Boba Tea (Variation)

I used the "ready in 5 minutes!!" tapioca pearls in this recipe. I tried to use the regular ones and it was a disaster and took forever, so I highly recommend the ones that are already partially hydrated. I found them at a local Asian market. Follow the directions on your package, but mine required 1 cup of pearls to be boiled in 10 cups of water for about 5 minutes. When pearls are done cooking, drain them and place them in a simple syrup (see recipe on page 251).

Boba Tea Mix

Makes 12 drinks

Blend ingredients in a Vita-Mix, using the accelerator tool to push the ingredients into the blades. Once powdered, remove and store in an airtight container until use. Since this is a homemade mix without any added anticaking agents, you may need to break up chunks with a spoon.

Boba Tea (Variation)

Makes 1 serving (increase as necessary)

step 1 Blend water or soy milk with boba tea powder mix until smooth. It'll mix nicely in a blender.

step 2 Place tapioca pearls in the bottom of a glass. Add ice to pearls. Pour strawberry mixture over ice and pearls, add straw, and serve!

Cheers to Delicious Drinks

Ingredients

Boba Tea Mix

$2^1/_2$ cups freeze-dried strawberries

2 cups freeze-dried ranbutans *(1 bag from Trader Joe's, or you can use other fruit—pineapple would be nice!)*

1 cup Better than Milk soy milk powder

1 cup sugar

Boba Tea (Variation)

$^3/_4$ cup water *(or soy or other milk if you prefer it super creamy)*

$^1/_4$ cup rounded boba tea powder mix *(from recipe above)*

$^1/_4$ cup *(scant)* prepared tapioca pearls

Chai Concentrate

4 to 5 1-inch cinnamon sticks

1 1-inch piece of ginger, roughly chopped (chop finer for stronger flavor)

$1/2$ teaspoon black peppercorns

2 points star anise (broken off)

6 to 8 cardamom pods, broken/smashed

$1/2$ teaspoon cloves

2 tablespoons black tea

4 cups water

Chai Boba Tea

$3/4$ cup chai concentrate (see recipe above)

2 to 3 tablespoons Simple Syrup (see recipe on page 251)

2 tablespoons Better than Milk soy milk powder

3 to 4 tablespoons prepared tapioca pearls

$1/2$ cup ice (if drinking cold)

Boba straws for drinking

Chai Concentrate for Boba Tea (Variation)

Here's the rule: 1 ounce of tea or tea mix to every 4 cups of water. You can do this with green tea, black tea, whatever! This is a chai variation.

Chai Concentrate for Boba Tea

Makes 4 drinks (easily doubled)

Feel free to play with this recipe. Change up the quantities to emphasize your favorite flavors. This one is a little cinnamon heavy because that's my favorite. Place all of the ingredients in a pot on the stove. Heat on high until boiling. Once it boils, begin timing. Let boil, covered, for 8 minutes.* After 8 minutes, immediately strain. Refrigerate until use or use immediately for hot boba tea.

*Note: Tea people. Don't wig out on me. Yes, you're boiling the leaves for 8 whole minutes. You're making a concentrate, so don't worry about activating the tannins in the tea. Once you add the sugar and soy milk powder for the drink, it won't be anywhere close to bitter, I promise.

Chai Boba Tea

Makes 1 drink (you can double, triple, etc.)

Combine first three ingredients, using a blender only if desired. If you're making it hot, you probably won't need a blender. It might be smoother if you use a blender for cold drinks. Add tapioca pearls to a glass, ice (if you're making a cool drink), and milky chai mix on top of that. Don't forget your boba straw. Serve.

Simple Syrup:

To make a simple syrup, put 1 cup of sugar and one cup of water into a medium-size saucepan and put on medium heat. Stir until the sugar is dissolved. After it has cooled, you can pour it into a glass jar and store it in the refrigerator to use in your boba tea recipes.

Simple Syrup

1 cup sugar

1 cup water

Ingredients

Horchata

Horchata needs to be prepared in advance, as the rice and almonds need to soak overnight before completing the drink. You also need cheesecloth or a nut milk bag to strain out the ground-up rice and almonds. It's a really delicious, creamy, cinnamony rice milk that is wonderful on a hot day.

Horchata

Makes 4 to 6 servings

step 1 Blanch almonds for 1 minute in boiling water and drain. Slip them out of their skins and place them into the bottom of a large pitcher.

step 2 Grind the rice in a blender or a spice mill into as fine a powder as possible. Add this to the pitcher.

step 3 Drop in the cinnamon stick and the lime zest, if using. Add 4 cups of the water and stir. Let this sit overnight in the refrigerator.

step 4 The next day, strain the mixture through several layers of cheesecloth or a nut milk bag into a large bowl, squeezing the milk out of the solids and discarding the solids. (I strained my mixture three times to remove as many particles as possible.)

step 5 Add the sugar and up to 3 cups more water and chill until ready to serve. Serve over ice!

Ingredients

2 cups almonds, blanched, with skins removed

1 cup white rice, long-grain

1 2-inch cinnamon stick

Zest of 1 lime *(optional)*

7 cups water

3/4 cup sugar

This a wonderful drink for a party or a late brunch after the party. You can use canned pears if you don't have fresh. Rosemary sprigs are a beautiful garnish. You can also substitute dried cranberries for cherries if needed.

254

Pear Cherry Bellinis

Makes 4 to 6 drinks

step 1 Pour 1 cup of boiling water over the dried cherries and let sit until the cherries are plumped and the water is colored and flavored, about 15 minutes. Strain the cherries, reserving the cherry water.

step 2 Add ³/₄ cup of the cherry water to a blender with the chopped pears, sugar, and lime juice until smooth.

step 3 Pour pear puree into champagne glasses, only filling half full. Add plumped cherries to each glass along with a sprig of rosemary. Just before serving, top off with champagne, sparkling water, or sparkling cider.

¹/₄ cup dried cherries, plumped in 1 cup boiling water

³/₄ cup cherry water *(reserved from soaking cherries)*

2 pears, peeled and cored

2 tablespoons sugar

1 tablespoon lime juice

Rosemary sprigs, for garnish

Champagne, sparkling water, or sparkling cider

Ingredients

Rosewater Lassi

This is a wonderful summer drink. Most lassis in the states are mango flavored. They're certainly delicious, but I prefer this more basic lassi, which has been sweetened and perfumed with rose water. If you want it to be a bit more exotic, add a pinch or two of cardamom.

Lassis were originally salty, and in decent Indian restaurants, you can order a salty lassi, sometimes flavored with roasted cumin. I'm not that brave, however, so I stick to the sweet variety. I've never seen a soy lassi on a menu, sweet or salty, so if you've never had one before, you should give it a try at home. They're great in hot weather or served with spicy foods.

Rosewater Lassi

Makes two 8-ounce servings

Blend all of the ingredients for several seconds. To make a cooler, icy treat, blend in 4 to 6 ice cubes at the end until smooth.

2 cups soy yogurt, plain or vanilla *(two 6-ounce containers, though less than 2 cups will also do)*

$^1/_2$ cup cold water

2 to 3 tablespoons sugar

2 teaspoons rose water

Pinch of cardamom *(optional)*

Ingredients

Meat from 1 Thai coconut *(also called a "young coconut")*

1/2 cup coconut water from above coconut

1/2 cup chai concentrate *(see recipe on page 250)*

3 tablespoons Simple Syrup *(see recipe on page 251)*

3 to 4 tablespoons tapioca pearls

Thai Tea with Fresh Coconut (Soy Free)

Makes 1 drink

Open coconut and strain off water into a bowl and set aside. With a spoon, scrape the meat from the inside of the coconut and put it in a blender. Add the tea concentrate, syrup, and coconut water and blend well until frothy and creamy. Add tapioca pearls to the bottom of a glass, add Thai tea mix (heated or with ice), and serve.

chapter ten

Sauces, Dips, and Spreads

Cranberry-Orange Sauce

hile I admit I love jelled, canned cranberry sauce, sometimes it's nice to whip up a fresh batch. You can add whatever flavorings you want (I like a little orange in it), and control the sweetness or tartness of the sauce. Most commercial brands contain high fructose corn syrup, so making your own sauce also has the advantage of being cane sugar- based. I like a chunky sauce every once in a while, but you can also mill the sauce to remove the skins and make a smooth, jelled sauce just like you'd get at the store.

Vegan Yum Yum

Cranberry-Orange Sauce

Makes 4 to 6 servings

Place all the ingredients in a saucepan. Boil for 10 to 15 minutes, or until thickened sufficiently. Refrigerate before serving.

2 cups cranberries

$1/2$ cup sugar

$1/2$ cup water

$1/4$ cup orange juice

Zest of 1 orange

Ingredients

Creamy Maple Sesame Dressing

This sweet dressing is well balanced and can be used on more than just lettuce. Try it as a dressing for a summer pasta salad with all your favorite veggies and a few hunks of tofu.

Vegan Yum Yum

Creamy Maple Sesame Dressing

Dresses 1 head of lettuce

Mix together the mayo, vinegar, sesame oil, mustard, maple syrup, salt, and pepper in a small bowl. Slowly drizzle the vegetable oil into the bowl while whisking vigorously to emulsify. The oil should blend completely into the dressing and it should thicken. Taste and adjust if necessary. Serve or refrigerate for up to three days.

$1\frac{1}{2}$ tablespoons vegan mayonnaise

$1\frac{3}{4}$ teaspoons balsamic vinegar

2 teaspoons toasted sesame oil

$1\frac{1}{2}$ teaspoons Dijon mustard

$1\frac{1}{2}$ tablespoons maple syrup

$\frac{1}{4}$ teaspoon salt

Fresh pepper, to taste

2 to 4 tablespoons mild vegetable oil *(canola, peanut, or light olive oil)*

Ingredients

Grilled Corn, Peach, and Tomato Salsa

This salsa is sweet and smoky and a wee bit spicy. After it sits, I'd say that it's about "medium" in terms of heat, so adjust accordingly. My tomatoes were pretty acidic, so you might want to use more vinegar if yours are more normal.

Grilled Corn, Peach, and Tomato Salsa

Makes 4 to 6 appetizer servings

step 1 Heat up a grill, indoors or outdoors. Indoors, I set it on medium-high.

step 2 While the grill is heating, prep the vegetables. Core the tomatoes and cut a small X on the bottom. Lightly oil them and place them on the grill. Shuck the corn, lightly oil it, and place it on the grill. Place the whole chilies on the grill.

step 3 Peel, halve, and pit the peaches and set aside.

step 4 Grill the vegetables for about 15 minutes, turning frequently. If you're using an outdoor grill, mind the tomatoes. If they get too soft, they'll melt right through the grates. Once all the vegetables have some coloring and are cooked, about 15 minutes, remove and let cool.

step 5 While the vegetables are cooling, grill the peaches for about 1 minute, then turn and grill for 1 minute more. Remove and let cool.

Ingredients

Oil for grilling

5 medium tomatoes

4 ears of "butter and sugar" corn *(or whatever kind is available)*

2 serrano chilies

3 small peaches

3 tablespoons olive oil

1 teaspoon balsamic vinegar

1 to 2 teaspoons lime juice

$1/2$ teaspoon salt

$1/2$ teaspoon cumin

$1/2$ cup fresh coriander *(cilantro)* or parsley, chopped

step 6 Once cool, halve the tomatoes and scoop the seeds and juices into a smaller, separate bowl (if you want a moister salsa, add the tomato juices; if not, discard the juices). Put diced tomatoes into a large bowl.

step 7 Remove the corn from the cob. If you have a Bundt pan, place the ear of corn vertically on the hole in the middle of the Bundt pan and use a knife to cut the kernels off—they will fall into the Bundt pan instead of getting everywhere. Place the corn kernels in the bowl with the tomatoes. De-seed the chilies, mince, and add to the bowl. Dice the peaches and add to the bowl.

step 8 Add the olive oil, vinegar, lime juice, salt, and cumin. Mix well, taste, and adjust seasoning. It will get spicier as it sits! Let it sit in the refrigerator for at least 30 minutes, but prepare no longer than 1 day in advance. Remove from the fridge, add fresh, chopped coriander (cilantro) and/or parsley, and serve with chips.

Roasted Eggplant and Caramelized Onion Marinara

When your regular pasta sauce just isn't doin' it for you anymore, make this.

2 eggplants, peeled, sliced into 1/4-inch discs, then cut into strips

1 teaspoon salt, divided

1/2 cup olive oil, divided

1 sweet yellow onion, diced or cut into half-moons

3 cloves garlic

1/2 teaspoon thyme

1/2 teaspoon basil

1/2 teaspoon oregano

1 28-ounce can tomatoes, diced or pureed

Black pepper

1 tablespoon Earth Balance margarine *(optional; for crazies like me)*

Salt for seasoning, up to 1 1/2 teaspoons

Roasted Eggplant and Caramelized Onion Marinara

Makes 4 servings, easily halved if cooking for two

step 1 Preheat the oven to 400°F.

step 2 Slice eggplants, peeled or unpeeled, into discs. Stack up some of the discs and cut them into strips until all the discs have been cut. Spread them out in more-or-less one layer on a paper-towel-lined cookie sheet—you can alternate layers of eggplant and paper towels if needed. Make sure each layer of eggplant is sprinkled lightly with salt. Let rest and remove the now-damp paper towels.

step 2 Coat the eggplant lightly in oil and bake for 20 minutes.

step 3 Meanwhile, add 1 tablespoon of the olive oil to a large skillet or pot. Heat, then add the onion and sauté over medium-high heat. In a few minutes, the onion should begin to color. Do not burn, but cook until very soft and caramelized, about 10 minutes (or longer).

step 4 Add the garlic, thyme, basil, and oregano and cook for 1 minute longer. Add the tomatoes, pepper, and margarine and stir well.

step 5 When the eggplant has baked for 20 minutes, use a long spoon to stir it up—it should be starting to brown and soften. Bake for an additional 10 minutes or until fully cooked, soft, and browned. If you want, you may add more oil at this point. When the eggplant is done, add it to the tomato sauce and stir well. Taste and add salt to your liking. (I put in 1 1/2 teaspoons more!) Serve over your favorite pasta immediately or refrigerate or freeze.

Sesame Soy Dressing

I created this dressing for the Pea Tendrils and Daikon Noodle Salad (page 129), but it's a great light dressing to be used over any salad you happen to be making. It's a savory rather than sweet dressing, a perfect contrast for sweet veggies like daikon, carrots, corn, and bell peppers.

3 tablespoons soy sauce

2 tablespoons soy milk

1 tablespoon toasted
sesame oil

1 tablespoon agave nectar

1 tablespoon apple cider
vinegar

1/4 teaspoon powdered
ginger *(or fresh to taste;
approximately 1 teaspoon)*

1 small dash cayenne
pepper

Black pepper, to taste

6 to 7 tablespoons canola
or peanut oil

Sesame Soy Dressing

Makes about 2 cups

Whisk together the soy sauce, soy milk, sesame oil, agave nectar, vinegar, ginger, cayenne pepper, and black pepper. Slowly drizzle in the oil while whisking vigorously, until emulsified. You can do this in a running blender or food processor if you prefer. Chill until ready to use.

Ingredients

Sweet Miso Salad Dressing

This is the salad dressing that got my husband to eat, and enjoy, salads. I whipped it up one morning while we were cooking for a holiday meal, so I can guarantee it's quick and easy to throw together, even as an afterthought. We never buy salad dressings anymore!

1 heaping tablespoon sweet white miso

1 heaping tablespoon Dijon mustard

1 tablespoon granulated sugar

1 teaspoon balsamic vinegar

2 pinches salt

Fresh cracked black pepper, to taste

3 to 4 tablespoons peanut or vegetable oil (your choice)

1 tablespoon hot water

Sweet Miso Salad Dressing

Dresses 1 head of lettuce

Put the miso, mustard, sugar, balsamic vinegar, salt, and pepper into a bowl. Use a whisk to mix the ingredients thoroughly. Slowly drizzle in the oil while whisking constantly, creating an emulsion. The dressing should turn shiny and thick. Taste and reseason if necessary. Whisk in hot water to thin, if needed. Let the dressing stand for a few minutes and whisk again before serving.

Tamarind Chutney

This is the perfect compliment to samosas (page 89), but it's great over tofu as well. Sweet and tangy with a little bit of spice, it's a real crowd pleaser.

2 cups water

2 tablespoons tamarind paste

1/2 cup sugar

1 teaspoon salt

1 teaspoon red chili flakes

1 teaspoon garam masala

1 teaspoon cumin

Tamarind Chutney

Makes 1/2 cup

In a small saucepan, bring the water, tamarind paste, and sugar to a boil. Let the mixture boil for 30 minutes until reduced and thickened. Add the salt, red chili flakes, garam masala, and cumin. Cook for 1 minute more, then remove from heat and let cool completely. Serve with Samosas (see page 89), or use in the tamarind tofu cabbage bowl recipe (see page 83).

Ingredients

Tangy Cashew Spread

This is kind of weird, but I like it. It's sweetish, tangy, and creamy. It's like mayonnaise but not. It doesn't really taste like mayo, but that's the sort of condiment it is. I put it on my seitan black bean burgers with some ketchup, and it was delish. It would also be a fun thing to dip fries in, like some strange vegan version of the European favorite (fries and mayo).

I used my Vita-Mix, but this will mix fine in regular blenders. If you're using your blender, try soaking the cashews overnight, which might soften them up a bit and make them blend more smoothly. This makes a great base, so adding fun flavors to customize your meal would be great. Possible additions for flavor are chili powder, wasabi, lime, garlic, dill—anything you can think of.

1³/₄ cups cashews

¹/₂ cup water

¹/₄ cup seasoned rice vinegar *(less if you're not a fan of tang)*

¹/₄ teaspoon salt

¹/₄ cup mild oil such as canola, peanut, or light olive oil *(or water for a lower-fat version; but if you're adding more water, use just enough so that the mixture will blend smoothly and still remain thick enough to spread, like mayo)*

Tangy Cashew Spread
Makes 1¹/₂ cups

Blend together the cashews, water, vinegar, and salt until smooth. Add the oil while the blender is running to emulsify. The mixture should be thick and creamy. Refrigerate until ready to use.

Ingredients

Vegan Worcestershire Sauce

I tasted bottled vegan Worcestershire sauce as I was making this recipe. My sauce is pretty close! It's not only cheaper to make than buying the bottles, but if you live in an area where vegan Worcestershire sauce isn't available, this will be a great stand-in!

1 teaspoon oil *(if using shallot/onion)*

1 shallot, chopped *(optional)* or ¼ cup chopped onions *(optional)*

1 clove garlic

1 cup water

¼ cup plus 1 tablespoon low-sodium tamari

2 tablespoons apple cider vinegar

2 tablespoons tamarind concentrate

2 tablespoons molasses

2 tablespoons sugar

1¼ teaspoons salt

1 teaspoon ketchup

5 cloves, ground, about ⅛ teaspoon

½ teaspoon chili powder

1 heaping tablespoon cornstarch

Vegan Worcestershire Sauce
Makes 1½ cups

step 1 If using the shallot/onion, heat the oil in a sauté pan and add chopped shallot/onions and garlic. Cook until softened, about 5 minutes, then put into a blender. If not using the onions/shallot, just put the raw clove of garlic into the blender or food processor and screw the whole cooking thing.

step 2 Add the water, tamari, vinegar, tamarind concentrate, molasses, sugar, salt, ketchup, cloves, and chili powder to a blender or food processor and whiz until well combined. Put the mixture into a small saucepan. Add just enough water to the cornstarch to make a smooth paste, then add to the sauce.

step 3 Heat for 5 minutes (or so) on high, whisking constantly, until the sauce is slightly thickened and glossy. Remove from the heat and refrigerate until cool.

Acknowledgments

There are so many people who worked on this book, I absolutely couldn't have done it without them!

Cathy—Whose life would have been a lot easier if all she had to do was dot my i's and cross my t's. Her work is invaluable.

Celine—Whose continued support means more to me than she knows.

My family—Who cheered me on every step of the way.

Sandy—Who never turned down a request to try a new recipe.

Stewart—The best husband in the world.

VeganYumYum Readers—Without whom this book wouldn't exist!

And of course, all my testers, who worked tirelessly to make these recipes the best they could be:

Erica Barraca, Thalia C. Palmer, Rose Hermalin, Zeyneb Akel, Laura Faye Berry, Angela White, Becca Bennett, Kim Carpenter, Amy Madden, Ashley MacDonald, Kelly Peloza, daphne haller, Mary Worrell, Martine v. Rooijen, Sarah Beck, Diana Jaramillo, Jule Jankauskaite, Ditte Johansen, Steffanie Smith, A. L. Alden, Catherine Pinon, Kate Matthews, Tami Noyes, Suzanne Rizzo, Evan McGraw, Kimberlee Redman, Anna Surbatovich, Raelene Coburn, Ashley Stephen, Shanell Dawn Williams, Amanda Sacco, Monica Matus, Marleigh Riggins, Vez Kirkpatrick, and all the other testers who did not wish their names to be printed here.

INDEX

A

B

drinks. *See* beverages

E

Easy Weekend Pancakes, 32–34

eggplant

Eggplant and Basil Stuffed Tomatoes, 96–98

Miniature Napoleons with Eggplant Creme, 99–103

Roasted Eggplant and Carmelized Onion Marinara, 267–68

Eggplant and Basil Stuffed Tomatoes, 96–98

G

garbanzo beans

Chana Samosas, 88–90

Golden Chickpea and Artichoke Salad, 121–22

ginger

Chinese Broccoli Wontons in a Ginger-Soy Broth, 166–70

Sesame Ginger Seitan Dumplings, 108–10

Glazed Green Bean Salad, 123–24

Gnocci with Thyme Vinaigrette and Lemon Cashew Cream, 190–94

Golden Chickpea and Artichoke Salad, 121–22

green beans

Glazed Green Bean Salad, 123–24

greens. *See* salads; *specific types of greens*

Grilled Corn, Peach, and Tomato Salsa, 264–66

Grilled Pear, Walnut, and Cabbage Salad, 125–27

H

Homemade Vegetable Stock, 175–77

Honeydew Coconut Tapioca, 232–33

Horchata, 252–53

Hurry Up Alfredo, 195–96

I

Indian dishes

Aloo Matar, 36–39

Chana Samosas, 88–90

Dal Makhni, 53–54

Rosewater Lassi, 256–57

Sheera, 242–43

Italian dishes. *See also* pasta

Eggplant and Basil Stuffed Tomatoes, 96–98

Italian Rice and Beans, 58–59

Italian Rice and Beans, 58–59

J

Japanese dishes

Onigiri, 104–7

Tanuki Soba with Spinach Tempura, 182–84

K

kale

Crispy Sesame Kale, 140–41

Lime Peanut Noodles with Seitan, Kale, and Carrots, 197–98

Marmalade Tofu with Kale and Lemon Pearl Couscous, 60–62

Pineapple Baked Tofu with Seared Pineapple Rings and Nutty Greens, 63–65

L

leeks

Carmelized Leek and Spaghetti Squash Polenta with White Sauce, 43–47

Potato Leek Soup, 178–79

Lemon Cranberry Muffins, 22–23

lemons

British Lemon Maple Scones with Clotted Cream, 7–9

Vegan Yum Yum

Vegan Yum Yum

Tofu Scramble with Seitan Sausage, 30–31

Tofu Scramble with Seitan Sausage, 30–31

tomatoes

    Creamy Tomato Barley Risotto, 138–39

    Eggplant and Basil Stuffed Tomatoes, 96–98

    Grilled Corn, Peach, and Tomato Salsa, 264–66

    Pan-Seared Tomato and Rosemary Artichoke Sandwich, 144–46

    Pasta Gremolata with Sun-dried Tomatoes and Garlic Bread Crumbs, 205–7

    Rigatoni with Fresh Grape Tomato Sauce, 210–11

    Roasted Eggplant and Carmelized Onion Marinara, 267–68

    Spicy Tomato Chickpea Soup, 180–81

    Super Quick Tomato Basil Cream Pasta, 216–17

troubleshooting

    for Crumpets, 21

V

Vegan Worcestershire Sauce, 277–78

vegetable dishes. *See also specific vegetables*

    Basic Vegetable Soup, 160–61

    Homemade Vegetable Stock, 175–77

    Moroccan Spiced Root Vegetable Home Fries, 142–43

    Vegetable Fried Rice, 84–86

    Velvety Vegetable Soup, 185–86

Vegetable Fried Rice, 84–86

Velvety Vegetable Soup, 185–86

W

walnuts

    Grilled Pear, Walnut, and Cabbage Salad, 125–27

Y

yams. *See also* sweet potatoes

    African Yam Stew, 158–59

About Lauren Ulm

Lauren Ulm, "Lolo," is a vegan foodie who lives in Boston with her husband and two cats. When she went vegan in 2004, the kitchen became her favorite room in the house and still is today. Her blog won the 2008 *VegNews* Veggie Award and the 2008 Veg Blog Award. She has appeared on *The Martha Stewart Show*, has been featured in *VegNews* magazine.

www.veganyumyum.com